FRESH
AND
SALT
WATER
SPINNING

The Barnes Sports Library

This library of sports books covers fundamentals, techniques, coaching and playing hints and equipment, uniformly priced at $1.50. Leading coaches and players have written these volumes. Photographs and drawings illustrate techniques, equipment and play.

BOOKS BY EUGENE BURNS

THE LAST KING OF PARADISE:
                       A Biography of Hawaii

THEN THERE WAS ONE:
           The Story of the USS Enterprise and the First
           Year of the War

FRESH AND SALT WATER SPINNING

The author, Eugene Burns, with a catch of trout.

FRESH

AND

SALT

WATER

SPINNING

BY
EUGENE BURNS

PHOTOGRAPHS
BY
CLYDE CHILDRESS

_____

_____

A. S. BARNES and COMPANY · NEW YORK

A WORD
TO THE
SPINMAN

FRESH AND SALT WATER SPINNING is dedicated to the proposition that the wise old fish, the old bruiser who has outmaneuvered a thousand anglers, can be taken most easily on spinning tackle. That's because, day in and day out, spinning takes more and bigger fish than any other method of sport fishing.

Whether you fish in fresh or salt water, this book will launch you on a never-ending quest of trophy fish in the comparatively heavily fished waters near your home.

But mind, it does not shout from the housetops the common refrain that you can learn to spin cast in twenty minutes—recognizing the absurdity of telling the beginning spinman that flinging a lure out a hundred feet will automatically produce big fish, although, admittedly, it occasionally does. Instead, *Fresh and Salt Water Spinning* is concerned with helping the angler get the best up-to-date equipment for his money; showing him how to cast delicately and accurately for the big fish; telling him how to read big fish water in stream, lake and ocean; instructing him how to fish this water effectively; helping him land the trophy fish; and finally teaching him how to build his own rod. As for the small fish, they are not our quarry. They come all too easily and are to be returned to get older, wiser and chunkier.

To the angler accustomed to heavier gear who may wonder, "What can I do with this 4½-ounce rod and 2-6 pound test line?" my answer is, "Wait until you've landed your first belly-sagging lunker—you'll be amazed how easily he is handled on your light, sporty tackle once you learn how to outwit him."

The spinning rod comes closest to being an all-purpose rod. With a plastic bubble you can pepper the water with a dry fly 75 feet away and drive trout absolutely nutty; with an independently lowered sinker you can deep-sea troll and take 30-pound salmon; with a heavier leader you can surf-fish and take stripers; with a heavier line on an extra spool you can cast a 5/8-ounce plug without a backlash and take heavy bass; with a light line you can cast your live bait farther than with any other outfit; and with a fly reel and a shooting line you can dry fly fish for brown trout or rainbow.

The spinning reel is responsible for this new type of fishing. Its stationary spool permits the use of almost invisible fine line and the placement of featherweight lures or live baits far out, beyond where fly or bait rod could put them. Better than this, though, is its adjustable friction clutch, which eliminates the two greatest hazards of big-fish angling: overstriking and overholding. Set the friction clutch slightly below the breaking strength of the weakest knot in your line and the friction clutch will do the rest, without fault.

Used properly with appropriate techniques, as outlined in *Fresh and Salt Water Spinning*, your outfit will produce about 80 per cent of the time—much higher than any other type of fishing.

Truly the angler who is embarking upon spinning and is determined to master this productive new method of fishing is to be envied. Once he masters his outfit, he will find himself trying new methods to help capture the biggest lunkers in near-by waters to paste on his wall. That makes for interesting fishing. Also, he will find himself constantly getting down to finer tackle which will give him the maximum play from the fish and give the fish the greatest sporting chance to break him.

Fresh and Salt Water Spinning was made possible by the groundwork laid in this country by such outstanding anglers as Bache Brown, Joe Bates, Al McClane, Joe Brooks, and George Thommen; by having such fine fishing friends as Charlie McDermand, Nate Buell, Claude Kreider, Rex M. Briggs, Francis E. Sell, Jay Long, and Dan Bailey, who, besides fishing, have the happy faculty of making an evening's campfire conversation even more interesting than the day's fishing; by getting the permission of the editors, Bill Rae of *Outdoor Life*, Jim Mitchell of *Hunting and Fishing*, and Hugh Grey of *Field & Stream* to recast material which I have prepared for their pages and some of the pictures which illustrated these articles; by having the technical assistance of Librarian Eloise Ryan; and, most important, by having the help of Clyde Childress, who made most of the photographs.

SAUSALITO,
CALIFORNIA

EUGENE BURNS
JUNE, 1952

CONTENTS

LIST
OF
ILLUSTRATIONS

FRESH
AND
SALT
WATER
SPINNING

I. EQUIPMENT

Wʜᴀᴛ's the best spinning outfit on the market today for the money?

What's the best technique to take big fish consistently on river, lake or ocean?

How can I recognize the "hot spot" in a stream? Lake? Ocean?

How can I land big fish on such light gear?

How can I build my own rod?

These five questions may seem like an abrupt way to start a book on spinning—but you're serious about spinning, aren't you? You don't want to waste time reading page after page about how an Englishman named Illingsworth developed the fixed spool back in 1905. All right then, let's get on to the main event.

First let's take up the question of spinning equipment. The others will be answered later in the book. But before you spend a dime on your new gear, may I suggest that you read this entire section on equipment—reels, rods, lines, lures? It may save you fully half the cost of your spinning outfit. Whether an angler likes to admit it or not, about 75 per cent of all his fishing gear gathers dust on the top shelf. For your own pleasure and profit, won't you decide right now, with the help of this book, to make your spinning outfit a long-term investment and get only what you need but make that the best you can possibly afford?

THE SPINNING REEL

The reel is the most important item of your spin fishing. On an average day's fishing it will make from 25,000 to 50,000 revolutions.

17

To stand up under such pressure, it must be well machined and durable. Therefore, get the best reel you can afford. You'll never regret it.

Basically there are three spinning-reel sizes, each appropriate to its job: (1) the small fresh-water reel, (2) the medium-sized reel for both fresh and salt water, and (3) the big-sized reel for salt water. To date, there is one beautiful small fresh-water reel; there are a dozen excellent medium-sized reels, and I know of no poor salt-water reel. See Figure 1.

Unless you are definitely committed to either deep-sea fishing or small-brook fishing, your first reel should be a good medium-sized reel which can be used for both fresh- and salt-water angling. Once you have practiced casting with such a reel and mastered it, you can specialize in either the larger or smaller sizes if you like. But get good reels. Not only will they give you more satisfaction but they will also give you more long-time, uninterrupted pleasant fishing.

Spinning began in Europe. As a result, the Europeans got the know-how of making good spinning reels. Eventually, I hope, we'll be able to make better and cheaper reels in America. But despite the import tax, the angler today can get a better dollar-for-dollar value in a European-made spinning reel.

Look for these qualities in your reel. They are listed, more or less, in order of importance:

An adequate line capacity; a delicate slip-clutch drag adjustment which will always stay the way you set it and deliver a smooth, uniform braking action; an easy, fast-opening bail or pick-up arm which will close automatically with the retrieve; an anti-reverse clutch (on medium-sized and larger reels) which will not permit the handle to turn backward while playing or netting a fish, or when trolling; a right handle if you are left-handed; cross level-winding to minimize tangled loop-casting; a long leg so that the line can "balloon" off the spool and into the gathering guide without slapping the rod; at least one extra spool for a different-sized line; a folding handle for convenient storage; and readily available parts replacements.

1

FIGURE 1. *There are many spinning reels on the market. The first two on the left, in the topmost row, are light reels particularly suitable to light rods and fresh-water angling. The remaining seven reels in the upper three rows are medium-weight and can be used for both fresh- and salt-water spinning. The bottom-row reels are comparatively heavy, with a large line capacity and intended for salt-water fishing. Reels from The Emporium, San Francisco.*

Before buying your spinning reel, test the slip-drag adjustment to see that it can be set precisely and that the setting neither slips nor changes tension while the spool rotates. Outside of the obvious spinning feature, this slip-drag clutch is perhaps the reel's greatest contribution to "fine and far-off" angling. If it is properly adjusted, the angler cannot overstrike his trophy fish or overhold him when he makes a run.

The anti-reverse is a splendid feature when tackling large game fish. In fighting large fish, it relieves the left hand from the unnecessary effort of "fighting" the handle, and when the fish "stops" and "gives," the handle may be wound with the lock remaining in the "on" position. By pumping—raising the rod and reeling in the slack line as the tip is lowered quickly—the line can be regained.

In the small, sweet-water class, the *Pecos, RuLac, C.A.P., Hardy,* and *Alcedo Micron* are ideal, particularly the last, which is Italian-made. For price, the *C.A.P.* will give the small fresh-water angler the best break. But how you'll love that jewel-like, tiny, *Alcedo Micron,* which can handle up to 135 yards of 3-pound test nylon mono-filament line. With experience, you'll even be able to handle steelhead on it.

In the medium-sized fresh- and salt-water field—from which you should make your first purchase, really—there are *Mitchell, Record, Pelican, Masterreel, Metro, Alcedo Omicron, Felton Crosswind, Monti, RuSport, Bradco, Bristol, SpinCast* and *Ambidex* to mention most of the leading makes. Swiss *Records* are made for either left- or right-handed anglers, and the British *Ambidex* and *Felton Crosswind* come with an interchangeable left- or right-hand crank. The *SpinCast,* made by the South Bend Bait Co., is a good buy but most spinning experts I know use the medium-priced French-imported *Mitchell.* I'll string along with them.

In the big salt-water class, the best reels are the *Centaure Ru-Mer,* large *Luxor, Ru-Atlantique* and the *Alcedo Lux Ormer,* which will soon be in production. Its Italian manufacturers have written to me that it will be the largest and lightest salt-water reel made, holding about 350 yards of 20-pound line and can be used either with the right or left hand. All of these reels are good. All are expensive.

THE SPINNING ROD

Before the spinman can select his rod impartially, a lot of inherited tradition must be abandoned.

Because spinning began in Europe, where most spinning was done with soft live bait in quiet water, a soft parabolic-action rod evolved. For a time, these soft rods were dutifully copied in this country and their proponents wrote many a treatise on their worth. Gradually, however, some more enterprising anglers found that a stiffer-action rod not only cast artificial lures more easily and more accurately but also gave the spinman greater distance with considerably less effort and wrist motion. So, inherited tradition took a nose dive and today's spinning rods are becoming longer and more stiff-tipped—in short, less like buggy whips. However, the soft rod is still the best for the man who uses live bait in slow water. (See Figure 2.)

The early rods, particularly the more expensive ones, were equipped with agate guides. It is now pretty well conceded that chrome-plated guides are harder, lighter, more wear-resistant, and they do not crack. So, out went agate guides. (Only recently, however, have some really well-engineered guides been introduced. To avoid needless repetition, these guides will be described in Chapter V, "Building Your Rod." Read it before buying your spinning rod because incorrect guides, improperly placed, can reduce your distance 30 per cent and vitally affect your accuracy.)

Again, flouting tradition, the long-accepted cork grip need not be more than 12 inches long. The 16- to 18-inch cork grips merely add from 4 to 6 inches of unnecessary cork and slow up the rod's action. Twelve inches allows ample space to shift the reel down to accommodate the lighter lures and line, or up higher for the heavier lures, besides giving you a chance to shove the butt of the rod against your belly for rest when playing a lunker. But see that the two reel bands fit snuggly around the cork grip. If a gap exists when they are new, they will eventually let the reel slip once the cork handle is worn. (Should this occur, use electric tape on the grip. Or as a temporary expedient, secure the reel with a pair of heavy rubber bands.)

The heavy 18-ounce, excessively long, European-made rods are outmoded and totally unnecessary—even though you can command a gillie to stand by your side. Besides, most medium-priced American split-bamboo rods are better today than any European rod ever was. For that matter, after a season's fishing in big water, there isn't a bamboo rod made, however expensive, which will compare in performance with today's modern hollow glass rods providing they are properly tapered. Besides, the glass rod can take much more punishment, needs far less care—a particularly good feature for salt-water fishing—and it will not take a set.

Before shopping for your spinning rod, settle these three points: With what other kinds of spinning gear—reel, line, and lure—will you use it? For what kind of fish? Under what conditions—weather and water?

Let's begin with the first point. With a light reel, light line, and light lure one would naturally say, "I'll pick a light, short rod." But wait. How does this fit with the kind of fish? With fishing conditions? Suppose the fish is a bull-dogging Dolly Varden rather than a fast-fighting rainbow. Obviously the heavy bull-dogging fish will require a heavier stick to bring him up. For open water, perhaps you'll want a longer one which will cast farther and play your fish better. If it is windy or the water has a swift current, you may wish a slightly heavier rod, although reel, line and lure remain much the same. If there are obstructions such as lily pads and logs, perhaps a still stronger and slightly heavier rod will fill the bill.

Now with a medium-sized outfit—say, a 4-pound test line and 1/4-ounce lure to go with your middle-weight reel—your all-purpose rod may well be a 7–7½-footer of 4½ ounces, with fairly stiff action. But yet, you may wish to do most of your spinning on an open lake where an extra 15 feet may be the big-fish-getting factor. Then, instead of a 7½-foot job you might want an 8-foot rod, or even go to 9 feet with a 5-ounce rod. (If you're an old-time spinman, don't smile indulgently at the rod's length. You'd be amazed, per-

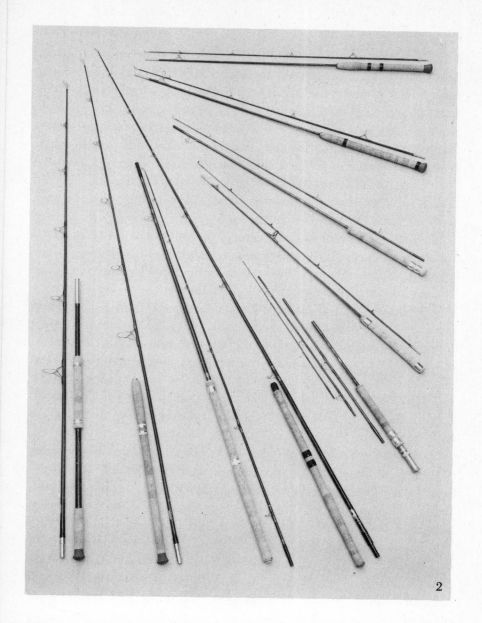

FIGURE 2. *These rods are representative of the many spinning rods on the market today. The lower four are two-handed rods used primarily for salt-water fishing or salmon and steelhead angling in fresh water. The upper four rods are principally for fresh water use. The little four-piece rod, in the middle, is a "back-packer"! Very handy for carrying up your sleeve, out of the house!* Rods from Spiro's, San Francisco.

haps, at how far such a rod will cast with the same effort, tradition notwithstanding.) But should the lake contain lily pads, you'd perhaps want a stronger, slightly shorter rod with more backbone, perhaps only 7½ feet. Should you be a soft-live-bait specialist, you might want a fairly long rod, but with a softer action from tip to butt—the English parabolic spinning rod, really—which would permit you to toss out a night crawler or a salmon-egg cluster without tearing.

Finally, let's consider the variations confronting the heavier-tackle spinman. In the salt-water class, with a heavier reel, he may wish a 9- or even 9½-foot rod from 5½ to 6 ounces. Perhaps even a two-handed, 10-foot rod of 8 ounces or better. The latter weight is satisfactory particularly where barnacles or sharp rocks necessitate a heavier line—although this too may be modified by using a heavier 20-foot-long leader ahead of the lighter line.

Reckoned by old-fashioned bamboo-rod standards, these varying specifications for light, medium or heavy salt-water rods might indeed have posed a most difficult problem, but with the advent of the modern hollow glass rod—the steel rod, too, although it is less adaptable—a much wider range of duties can be performed by one rod! Regardless of load, the glass rod will neither set nor break. Its proven power, resiliency, lightness and long-lasting qualities are truly remarkable.

As with other refined types of fishing, the beginning spinman will hear a lot of loudly proclaimed nonsense about "balanced" equipment. There is no such thing as balance in a spinning outfit, really. Change lure or line or reel or current or wind and what happens? Poof, away goes your imagined "delicate balance." And who knows what happens to balance when a big fish swings on. Instead of "balance," look toward matching your outfit so that it will efficiently perform the job to be done. With light reel, use light rod, light line and light lure when possible. So doing will assure more pleasure.

With a heavier line to hold a heavier fish, you'll need a heavier lure to take the line out for distance, and a heavier rod for enough power to cast it, with a heavier reel to accommodate the heavy line—but even with these "heavier" items, keep as close to the lighter side as possible—and to hang with "balance." With heavier gear, casting can become most burdensome by the end of the day, and then fishing pleasure is gone.

As for length in a spinning rod, get the longest rod possible consistent with minimum weight and maximum strength—because the longer rod usually adds distance. Yet, be sure the rod is short enough to have a fairly stiff butt and that its tip does not quiver after you stop your forward cast. A quivering tip kills distance. It holds back the line as it spins through the guides, and stops the lure, mid-air. So, before buying a spinning rod, press the butt against your belly and oscillate the rod back and forth. Then stop, quickly. If the rod's tip continues to vibrate, try another, until you find one that stops quickly.

In this inspection, sight through the guides, too. Except for the largest gathering guide, which must stand farther off the rod than the others to eliminate line-slap, the graduating guides should look like a diminishing cone.

Select your salt-water rod, too, primarily for the job to be done. Choose your rod to handle the line and lure and not some chance-passing big-shot whale. All too frequently the angler feels that the great ocean demands much heavier tackle—but even here, extremely heavy tackle is definitely not necessary. However, quite often in casting for stripers, blues or bonefish, long casts are in order—and weighted flies particularly are not the easiest lures to fling out a long distance with a light rod. Some of my experienced salt-water friends prefer 10-foot, double-handed, 8-ounce rods. I get more concentrated pleasure from a one-handed 9-foot, 5½-ounce stick, which meets most of my salt-water obligations—providing it is made of hollow glass. And, when I'm deliberately fishing for smaller fry—fish such as snappers, blues, or mackerel—I'll string along with my medium-weight trout spinning rod of 7 feet and 4½ ounces.

Should the angler like a spinning rod for back-packing or carrying past the boss in an innocent-appearing suitcase, then by all means get a three-section rod. In the bamboo, *Gene Edwards'* three-piece rod cannot be surpassed. In glass, you may want to get the *Sila-flex* or *Researchers Universal* blanks from the R. L. Winston Rod Co., 684

Harrison Street, San Francisco, Calif., and make it up yourself after you have read Chapter V. I have yet to find a good spinning and dry-fly rod combination which will surpass my own homemade job.

For a commercially built bamboo rod, I think my *Phillipson* is perhaps the best buy for the money. You can't go wrong with a *South Bend* in the medium-priced field. For the more expensive rods, you'll get full value in every *Edwards, Leonard, Thomas* or *Payne*. The same goes for the *Orvis*, which features a plastic impregnation which renders it waterproof and eliminates varnish. *Uslan's* five-sided rods have much to commend them.

For a general all-purpose beginner's rod to go with the *Mitchell* reel for both fresh and salt water, I would select a good glass rod of 7 feet and 4½ ounces. Good glass rods are made by *Conolon, Shakespeare, Harnell, Researchers Universal, Heddon* and *South Bend,* and all will give satisfaction.

For an ultra-light rod to go with my *Alcedo Micron* reel, I've got a 2½-ounce *Researchers Universal* hollow glass rod, 7 feet long, which not only has the power but also a tip stiff enough for dry-fly casting—something I'm not happy without because I am addicted to dry-fly fishing when the fish are surface feeding.

For a slightly heavier outfit than my medium job, I'd get a 7½- to 8½-foot glass rod of 4½ to 5 ounces; and for steelhead, if it required long casting in swift water during heavy weather, I'd get a 9-foot rod right around 5½ ounces.

THE SPINNING LINE

Spinning never could have made its rapid advance in this country without benefit of today's excellent spinning lines which grew out of du Pont's nylon—an answer to the spinman's prayer.

Three good types of spinning lines exist: the newly-developed platyl, Flexon or nylon monofilament; braided nylon monofilament; and braided nylon. Each of these performs a specific function in matching line to conditions—and where one will do a particular job to perfection another may actually be a handicap. Therefore the spinman must know his lines. And under no circumstances let a salesman palm off a non-spinning line for spinning under the pretext that "it's just as good!" Only a spinning line is a spinning line, no ifs, ands, or buts, and each spinning line has its limitations.

Since the weight of the lure must pull the line from the reel, the spinning line must offer the least resistance possible in getting off the spool and through the guides to extract a good cast. For best and easiest casting the line must be reduced to the absolute minimum in diameter because weight and thickness of line are arch enemies of distance. Stiffness or a tendency to coil also are handicaps. Yet, the line must have maximum strength for its diameter to withstand snapping off the lure by casting and to hold and tame the wild fish in fast water once the hook is in him. For continued performance, the line must also resist wear and deterioration.

Because the spinman will inevitably fall into the clutches of a "pioneer" spinman, I feel duty-bound to prepare the angler for his onslaught. He'll come at you with this opening: "Brother, let me tell you, you don't know how good you've got it today with all this new spinning gear on the market. Why, when I started threadlining (spinning, today), I had to soak my line overnight in a mixture of water and castor oil (glycerine was used by the more imaginative) and then keep it under wraps until I got to the stream, to keep the line moist and pliable." The only response is to remind him how good the "pioneers of the sport" had it in comparison to the West Coast Siwash Indian who used an abacus-like hand-held contraption and a home-made line made either of fiber or sinews!

Before proceeding, a point on line tests must be clarified. American lines usually test higher than their indicated breaking strength. European lines, on the contrary, are usually accurate. When they say a line is 2 pounds they mean just that. Hence some European lines, although their diameter is quite a bit smaller, have fallen into considerable disrepute because their indicated 2-pound test does not measure up to the heavier-diametered American "2-pound" test lines which actually should have been labeled anywhere from $2\frac{1}{4}$- to 3-pound test.

Although du Pont has some new stronger fibers in the "works," the strongest diameter for diameter spinning line available today seems to be platyl, a German importation. It's what the doctor ordered for spinning—completely limp and extremely pliable, making for smooth and longer casts, besides practically eliminating coiling and springing from the spool.

Nylon monofilament, also extruded in single filament, is almost as good in the lightweight tests—say from 2 to 6 pounds. Monofilament lines do not fray, split or get brittle. Besides, they are cheaper. But sad to say, the more expensive French nylon monofilaments are better than domestic ones: they are more pliable, softer, less stretchy, and for diameter size, have a higher test strength.

In the medium test lines, say from 4 to 12 pounds, braided nylon monofilament is best. It is hard, but fairly pliable, and shoots wonderfully well. Its one disadvantage is that it is hard on the guides.

In the heavy tests—over 8 pounds—primarily for deep-sea fishing, which sometimes entails casting a 3-ounce weight, braided nylon, consisting of many more threads than the braided nylon monofilament, is preferred by many casters who say that other lines tend to be too stiff in the heavier tests.

For comparative strengths in the 2-pound tests, where every ounce counts, these are the approximate diameters listed by the manufacturers: American .004 inch; French nylon (Tortue) .003 inch; platyl .0025 inch.

In fishing in unobstructed water with light test lines, a leader is unnecessary—nylon monofilament or platyl is leader enough. However, where obstructions exist such as sharp rocks, lily pads, and logs, it behooves the angler to barrel-knot on a 3-foot leader of slightly heavier line. In ocean fishing, where there are barnacles, sharp rocks, and tidal reef flats, bend on a longer leader—even up to 20 feet. For the tooth-filled jaws of the muskellunge or pike use a 6-inch length of fine braided wire leader attached to the line by a snap.

When going after large fish such as steelhead and salmon, it is not necessary to change to heavy "distance-consuming" line. Simply keep your reel threaded with 4- to 6-pound test monofilament and tie to the end of it a 6-foot trace of 6- to 8-pound test monofilament. This trace will enable you to land the majority of your large fish without line breakage because most of the strain is exerted on the first 4 feet or so of your line.

Where length of backing is not an important factor, the angler can save himself money by using a cheaper though heavier braided nylon backing. When length of backing is most vital, as in bone-fishing—where the fish may open the contest with an 800-foot sprint—splice in an even slightly lighter line, because the strain is never so great here as it is toward the front of the line due to friction in pulling through the water. With this finer backing, the spool will hold more line.

The smaller the line's diameter, of course, the less visible it is to the fish. Therefore, under difficult fishing conditions, where the water is hard-fished, clear and low, the lighter-equipped angler will usually take more of the larger-sized fish—providing skill and knowledge are part of his backing. As for line color, that's largely a matter of taste—and endless debate. My preference is a light-colored line which matches the underside of a fish—white shading into blue. Nature's own camouflage is good enough for me, and if she uses that color for the belly of fish there must be a reason for it.

For your first spinning line to go with your medium-sized reel and rod, get 4-pound test platyl, Flexon, or French monofilament (T-line, Tortue, Mitchell, or Water Queen). Of these, I prefer platyl. Then, carry two extra spools—the first loaded with lighter-weight line, say 3-pound test platyl; and the second with heavier, 6-pound test braided monofilament with short lengths of 8-pound test and 12-pound test leader material should you wish to go after the largest of fresh-water game fish. On any fishing trip, these two extra spools are always mighty fine insurance.

For your ultra-light outfit, get a 2-pound test line. For the extra deep-sea outfit, a 12-pound test braided nylon line. Before attaching line to spool, read the section on knots in Chapter II and then use the new knot which tests 99 per cent! See Figure 3 for the correct way of attaching line to spool.

To avoid excessive wear and weakening your line, do your practice casting on your lawn with an old line. In spinning every ounce counts and the knife-edged grass unfortunately plays hob with your fine line, wearing it down even faster than cement or gravel!

PRODUCTIVE LURES

No other method of fishing offers such a bewildering array of lures. By using weights, and the proper rod, reel and line, the spinman can handle just about every fishing lure made, from a tiny No. 18 Cahill dry fly to a 3-ounce salt-water jig!

When American spinning started, it was largely confined to European lures. Despite their deadliness in Europe, they proved only moderately attractive to most American trout and salmon and downright repulsive to our bass, walleyes, pike and panfish. Even that stout Continental standby, the *Devon minnow*, could only be depended upon to produce cannibal browns with fair consistency. There are exceptions: the *Preska spinner*, some of the spoons, and for baits the *Vaironnette minnow gang* were effective.

Today many spinning lures are being made in this country by reputable manufacturers—but, beware! A lot of improperly designed lures are being made by others who slipped aboard the gravy train.

Once again—it must be a familiar refrain by now—base your lure selection upon your specific fishing problem—consider the wind, water, fish you go after, and your other casting gear. And because the fish's appetite is involved, it might be in good taste to consult his dietary preferences by offering him a variety of lures until he finds what he likes. One day you'll find he prefers wobblers; another, minnows; while on a third, nothing, absolutely nothing at all!

In selecting lures, stick pretty close to those which get down to the bottom of the stream where the big fish hang out and do most of their feeding. But even so, use lures as light as possible and lines which are fine. The success of these smaller, lighter lures over the old-style, bulky, noisy plugs is already pretty well established. The nearly noiseless, smaller lures, which strike the water softly, have a far greater big-fish score. But keep in mind, too, the casting distance desired and the lure's wind resistance. Occasionally these considerations will call for a heavier lure—but a heavy lure's flight can be canceled by a vibrating rod tip. A light lure, too, can be slowed by a heavy line. (See Figure 4.)

Lure design is extremely important. The better lures alight in the water gently and without fouling; they do not twist the line—or

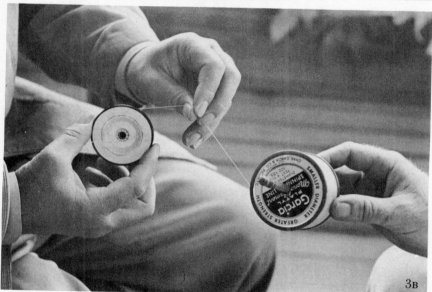

FIGURE 3.   *To put your line on the spool, get someone to hold the spool of line on a pencil, and apply a bit of pressure as you roll on ten turns, holding the reel spool by the back flange (3A); then reverse and roll on (3B) ten more turns. Count them. (Some reels, like Mitchell, wind counterclockwise.) Continue winding alternately, thus avoiding a twist in your line, until you have filled the spool evenly to the curve of the lip—but don't cut it, just yet. Tie the end of the line to a limb and run out the entire reel's spool, winding it in again with the handle to get the proper cross-winding effect. Now, if you need more line, or less, you can make the proper adjustment. Then cut it off.*

if they do they are made in pairs for left- and right-hand counter-acting twists; they are compact enough to give both distance and accuracy to the cast by lessening air resistance. Besides this, they attract fish consistently. Some lure faults can be minimized once the angler has gained experience. Lifting the rod and holding the lure just out of the water on the retrieve allows the line to untwist. A keel or rudder placed in front of an offending lure will usually eliminate line twist—though often it impairs the lure's action. (It is better to use pairs of opposite-turning lures.) Halting the lure just before it hits the water will sometimes straighten the hooks out behind it.

Few things are more disconcerting than getting a cast off to a promising start, only to have it skid a dozen feet off the target when it descends, due to a gusty wind. But the benefit accruing from a wind-slicing lure that casts like a bullet can be more than offset by its poor fish-taking ability. However, the *Wob-L-Rite* proves the exception. It casts well and takes fish. On steelhead in particular the ½-ounce Wob-L-Rite is a proven killer.

When water conditions are difficult—that is, when the water is low, clear and warm—a flashing lure will sometimes attract fish. On dark days, particularly. A bright lure has the further advantage of letting the spinman know exactly where it is in the water and it there-fore helps him make the proper alterations in speed and depth of retrieve. To keep it shining bright, polish the blade frequently. Hint: Do not touch the blade with your oily finger tips or you will dull its lustre immediately.

Get the habit: change lures often. It is all too easy to go on fishing, doggedly, determinedly, hour after hour, with the same lure because on the same stretch of water it once worked miracles. Take time out, sit down, and study your problem—and change lures. Even-tually you'll work out the taking combination.

Speaking of combinations, occasionally you'll get big fish to come out of hiding and follow your lure—but yet refuse to make contact. Suppose you are using a Colorado spinner. Retrieve again, quickly snap on a *Plucky*—which is an imitation minnow bait—and let him have it. All of it. Should the fish succumb to your ruse, don't continue with the Plucky. Go back to your winning combination. Use

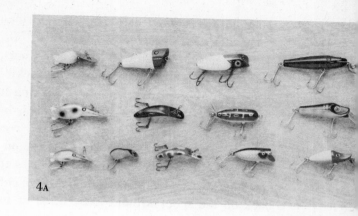

4A

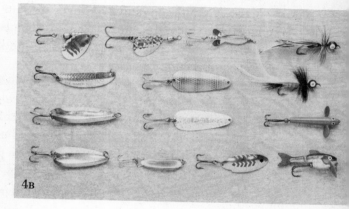

4B

FIGURE 4. *There are perhaps a thousand different spinning lures on the market already, with a score added every month. Many are poor but those shown on this page are proven fish-getters. They fall, roughly, into three classes: surface lures (4A, top panel); light subsurface lures (4B, middle panel); and heavy subsurface lures (4C, bottom panel). No other method of fishing permits such a vast assortment—from feather-light flies to be fished with a bubble to heavy deep-running lures. Live baits, too, can be fished effectively. Light subsurface lures (4B) can be fished near the surface or on the bottom, depending upon the current and the rate of retrieve. The flies are weighted. Heavy subsurface lures (4C) are usually easier to cast into the wind and give greater distance. They must be fished in comparatively fast water or retrieved quite quickly to keep from foul-hooking the bottom.* Lures from The Emporium, San Francisco.

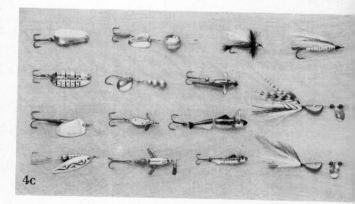

4C

the Colorado spinner as a come-on and then administer the *coup de grâce* with your deceiver.

To meet changing fishing conditions, the effective spinman usually has his lures arranged in his tackle box as: surface-working lures; subsurface lures; and deep-working lures.

Among the surface lures are flies, bugs, frogs, poppers and plugs. By keeping the rod tip high and reeling quickly, the jointed minnow imitations can be kept almost on the surface, too. When using popping bugs or other surface lures for bass, work them in fits and starts, with plenty of action. But take care that your line is wound back on the spool without loose turns or loops. The best way to do this is to maintain an even pressure on your line by letting it run between the thumb and forefinger of your rod-holding hand. How to handle surface flies, wet flies, salmon eggs, night crawlers, and other soft lures on a bubble is so important and new that it is discussed in a special section in Chapter II.

Subsurface lures usually produce best in comparatively shallow water. Most big fish are taken in a stream when the lure is worked fairly close to the bottom. A consistent rule is: Go deeper to root out the lunkers. Good subsurface lures are bucktail or beaded lures, wet flies, weighted flies, plugs, Creek Chub pikies, streamers and spinners. The Preska may weigh only ⅛ ounce, can be handled nicely in most waters as it does not have the tendency to sink too fast. But like all headless spinners, it will eventually twist the line unless a centerboard head is used.

The impact of most standard lures in shallow water will send fish scurrying for foxholes. Under such conditions, a small light-weighted spinner can be effective—say, a ⅒-ounce job with a silver blade and a brass-bead body. Hold the small blade almost stationary in the current and steer it slowly through every fishy-looking pocket—around rocks, undercuts and obstructions. Slowly. Always pause, hopefully, a minute or two in such likely spots. Out of seemingly barren water this teasing action may bring a reluctant behemoth.

It is the deep-water angler, however, who fishes under the heaviest currents—we'll go into this much more fully in Chapter III, "Fish and Water"—who usually picks up the trophy fish. This water should be the prime target of the spinman.

Among the deep-running lures are the spoons, wobblers, weighted lures, plugs and the heavier spinners. The wide Colorado blade will put rainbow, cutthroat and land-locked salmon consistently on the end of your line, and this blade will also spell the demise of many a bass, pike and perch. Most large fresh-water lunkers go for wobblers in a big way, and I have found that some of the Norwegian and Swiss wobblers with red stripes or red and black dots deliver. On one memorable trip, my deep-working *Abalone Killer* performed miracles in fish seduction. *Flatfish*, which are in. the same league, will frequently give a good account—but how I detest that array of fouling hooks.

Weighted flies, with lead wound around the hook's shank under the body dressing, or the more recently invented head-weighted streamer-tailed optics give good action and produce well. Streamers and bass-sized wet flies should also be in the spinman's kit.

For consistent fish-taking lures, my vote goes to the wobbling spoons. Their fluttering, wobbling, dive-and-dart action makes them universal attractors and deceivers. But besides the heavy type of spinning and wobbling lures, carry some thin-bladed spoons for medium-depth water and have some really heavy blades to cut through swift or fast-flowing water and to get down to the bottom.

Salt-water fish, unlike the fresh-water species, usually prefer lures that move fairly straight through the water. Faster, too. You may occasionally "jig" the lure with a short stroke of the rod. But many good fish are taken by letting the lure drift and sink with the current, using no rod action. For them, the weighted bucktail or jig produces fairly consistently.

As for the hook, whenever possible I change trebles to singles—putting on a Siwash hook which is preferred by many commercial fishermen. Besides permitting the harmless release of small fish, the single hook actually takes more fish. With a light spinning rod and an elastic line, it is difficult to set a large treble hook beyond the barbs at 75 to 100 feet unless the fish does it himself. A single hook sets again as easily beyond the barb. Besides, if you are using a large treble hook, you're using a large lure and a heavy line—all of which tend to alert and warn the wise old curmudgeon. By getting down to single hooks and finer tackle, you'll frequently have the old Wisenheimer impaled before he's aware of your duplicity—and if the small hook is needlepoint sharp, as it always should be, you'll set it more easily beyond the barb. With a light lure, the big fish will also be less likely to yank it out when he threshes about and goes into his aerial twistings—but there will be much more of this in Chapter IV, "Trophy Fish."

Depending upon fishing conditions, the following list will give the spinman a fairly well-rounded selection:

Small spinners from 1/16 to 1/10 ounces with light impact for shallow water
Small wobblers, same weight, for the same purpose
Small thin-bladed wobbling spoons, 1/4 ounce, for swift or deep water
Heavy-bladed wobbling spoons, 1/4 ounce, for swift or deep water
Surface minnows, about 1/4 ounce, for surface action
Weighted bucktails or jigs, about 3/8 ounce, for salt water
Selection of dry and wet flies for bubble fishing
Selection of weighted optic flies and bass flies
Light plugs and jointed lures from 1/8 to 3/8 ounce for all-around fishing.

Naturally, few spinmen will fish enough water to warrant getting this full battery of fish-killing lures and the angler should eliminate those which are not appropriate to his water—yet he must beware of a besetting danger which afflicts most anglers: the inclination to confine themselves to lures whose action and purpose is nearly the same.

In addition to reel, rod, lines and lures, the spinman's accessories are comparatively few. He should have snaps to attach lures to line quickly, swivels and rudders to eliminate line twist, short wire leaders for sharp-toothed fish, plastic bubbles, extra hooks of various sizes, weights, assorted leader material, a small hook sharpener, a blade-polishing cloth, and oil for swivels—they function much better when oiled.

It is false economy to cram your lure box so full of lures that you have a hard time deciding which one to use—but it is false economy, too, to spend time and money getting to your favorite fishing spot, and yet be too underequipped with lures to exploit it. That which stamps the efficient, experienced angler is the appropriateness of the gear he carries and the small amount of fishing tackle he leaves to collect dust on his shelves.

II. TECHNIQUE

HOW TO CAST

Within thirty minutes the beginning spinman should be able to cast well enough to take fish occasionally. However, as with anything deceptively easy, there are refinements—and these are the ones which produce heavy fish.

Let's be about our spinning. Put up your rod. Attach reel, pendulum fashion, spool forward, on the underside of your rod handle. Align the reel with the guides and secure the reel base firmly with the two movable rings. Having the reel handle on the left may feel awkward for the first ten minutes but once so used, it will prove convenient and pleasant. See Figure 5 to learn how to handle the friction drag, and Figure 6 to learn how to make the lure enter the water properly. For the preliminaries to casting also see Figure 6.

Before you cast, make a few practice swings. Stand comfortably, relaxed, facing the target. Put your right foot slightly forward. With your eyes and mind fixed on a spot 2 feet above the target, make a few overhead swings with your rod through a 75-degree arc, from 10 o'clock to 12:30 and 12:30 to 10, without stopping the rod at the upward position. If you stop at the 12:30 position more than a moment, you will lose the power that is built up and compressed into the flexed rod during that backward drive. Now work this forward-backward action into a rhythmical, pendulum-like swing—coming back fairly fast, driving forward faster—and stopping the forward

5

FIGURE 5. *Before making your first cast, experiment with your friction drag on the reel until it is set exactly right—slightly below the breaking point of your weakest knot. When fishing with that line and knots, never change your setting. Trust your friction drag implicitly unless the fish makes an unusually long run, then release it slightly to compensate for the line drag.*

power application near 10 o'clock, yet drifting through to 9:30 o'clock
with your follow-through for accuracy. Now, do it again, but pause
this time just an instant on the back swing to give the lure slightly more
time to straighten out behind you and pull on the rod. Keep at it until
this action comes easily out of your wrist, smoothly and naturally.

You've got it. Good. Let's begin casting. (See Figures 7 to 9.)

Because you will tend to release the line too soon, your first
few casts may go almost straight up. (If you release too late they
will slam down in front of you.) Don't let a few poor casts upset
you. By determining the release point, you'll be on it soon. Then, by
judging the flight of the lure and braking the reel at the right instant,
your distance will be in hand before you know it. But don't try for
distance: that will improve automatically with your timing.

With lighter lures, your back cast must be made stronger and
faster; with heavier lures, slower and easier. The lighter the lure,
the greater the distance it should hang from the tip top. A dangling
lure, when cast, will travel in a greater arc, thereby increasing its
momentum for greater distance and casting ease. Thus, with the same
rod, the same line, and the same reel setting on the cork grip, you'll
soon be able to cast quite a variety of lures easily.

For a modification of your overhead cast, change the plane
from overhead to 45 degrees. Soon you may find yourself using this
cast almost exclusively. Its method of execution is exactly as the
overhand cast—merely tilt the rod. The advantage of this cast is that
it keeps the lure traveling in a flatter trajectory which will give the
wind less chance to pull it off its course and allow it to drop into
the water more gently. With more wind, you'll want to get it even
more horizontal.

There are four more casts but they come under the head of
"trick" shots. (See Figures 10 and 11.) They should be mastered
because they can put your lure in unfished spots, and unfished spots
are where lunkers frequently congregate to scoff at frustrated anglers.

To slow up the lure mid-air with your many casts is wonderfully
easy. Merely drop the tip of your right index finger gently on the line
or against the edge of the spool. Gentle does it. At any time, of
course, a sudden pressure against the spool will stop the lure dead

6A

FIGURE 6. *To take up the slack and slow your lure gently, mid-air, drop your index finger and let it touch the "ballooning" line. Then, when the lure is just inches above the target, touch the spool gently (6A,* top). *By raising the rod tip at this exact instant, you can make the lure slip-dive into the water. To prepare to cast, first reel in your lure within 8 inches or so of the tip top. Bring the pick-up finger to the top of the reel and catch the line on the middle of the ball of your index finger, ahead of the first joint (6B). While holding the line across your index finger tip, take hold of the shell and turn it back so the pick-up arm is at the bottom of the reel. Still holding the line with your index finger, open the pickup or bail (6C,* lower right) *and you are ready to cast.*

6B

6C

FIGURE 7. *Once the overhand cast (7A, top) is mastered, the others will come easily. Study the figure of my friend, Rex Briggs, then align your rod with a spot which is exactly 2 feet above the target from a 10-o'clock position with the ¼-ounce lure dangling 6 inches from the tip top. You should be comfortable, relaxed. The reel should be ready for casting with the pick-up finger open. The line should be under the ball of your right forefinger tip. Concentrate upon that spot 2 feet above the target. Bring the rod back fast from A to B, and while the rod is flexed backward, drive forward twice as fast, hesitating just the briefest instant between the two motions until the line is pretty straight behind. As your line comes forward to the 10-o'clock position, let the line slip off your finger tip. Your line will shoot out like a bullet. For accuracy, follow through by sighting 2 feet above the target while lowering the rod to 9:30, coming to rest at C. Stop the lure over the target by dropping the forefinger on the reel spool. To cast a bass bug or a weighted popper from 40 to 60 feet with accuracy and to make your desired splash, start the rod from a 3-o'clock position behind you (7B), then sweep it forward overhead, using a little wrist snap to build up additional power. Release at 11 o'clock, following through to 9:30 for accuracy.*

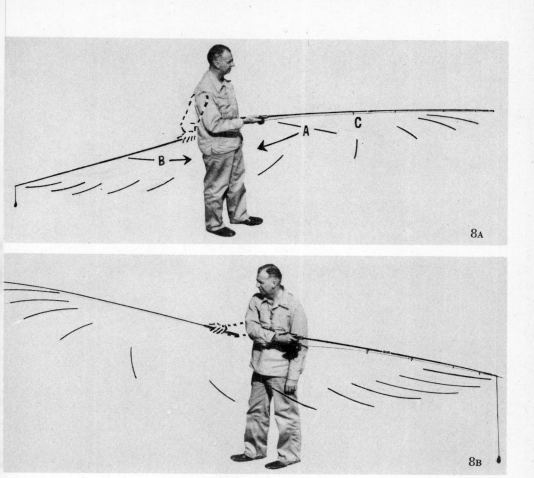

8A

8B

FIGURE 8. *To deposit the lure gently under some distant foliage, the overhand cast used in a horizontal plane (8A) will work wonders. Although it is not so accurate as the overhead, the same cocking of the rod from 10 to 12:30 takes place—exaggerated in the photo-diagram due to the camera's angle—and the release, again, is at about 10 o'clock with a 9:30-o'clock follow-through. With practice, this cast can be effective at a distance, and it works well to get under wind. To cast a heavy lure, while not putting any undue strain on your light rod, the side cast is most accommodating (8B). In this cast the lure dangles about 30 inches from the tip top. Begin the cast from almost directly behind you, and with an easy upward swinging motion of about 15-degree climb, aim your tip out and up. Release the line as your swing reaches the highest point and the maximum speed. The proper timing of the release brings this cast off. If this cast with a heavy lure is not smoothly delivered, you will end on your knees on the far bank, searching in the grass for your catapulted lure. Execute this cast either forehand or backhand.*

FIGURE 9. *With the very lightest of spinning lures it is possible to add any-where from 10 to 15 feet by making a combination under- and overhand cast (9A). Let the lure dangle from 30 to 36 inches. Sweep it back with a sidearm job. Come forward, without pausing, in an overhand cast. Reach well up as you finish off your cast so that your hand, holding the rod, is about 30 inches beyond your face. In this cast, the lure will describe a rising half circle before it leaves the rod. The intent is to get distance with only the lightest of lures. For soft baits, a shallow "U" cast imparts a smooth delivery which will take the bait out without injury (9B). Begin the cast behind you with a sidearm, almost as high as your shoulder. As you bring it forward, pouring on power, dip it down, and then raise it again almost to shoulder height before releasing it so that it will float out without even a suggestion of a jerk. This will give distance to even the softest of baits—something no other piece of tackle yet devised can impart.*

in its flight. But do this with discretion unless you have an unlimited supply of lures.

Wind presents ugly problems to the light-lure addict. When casting into the wind, get as low to the water as you can with the side cast, either from the right or left side. The solution is: Keep line and lure traveling in the flattest trajectory possible. Stop the lure in flight to take the wind-blown belly out of the gossamer line.

That which sets the accomplished spin angler apart from the mere distance caster is the attainment of accuracy and unbelievable delicacy in depositing the lure on the water with a slip-dive finish. With the delicate angler, the lure will barely spat the water, and will get to work immediately. The trick, of course, is to extract the momentum from the lure inches above the water. To do this, slow up the lure's flight when it is still in the air by touching your index finger to the "ballooning" line. Then, when the lure is just inches above the target, kill it dead. By raising the rod tip at this exact instant, you can make the lure slip-dive into the water. To put the lure to work as soon as the blade bites into the water, begin to turn the handle of the reel slowly with the left hand just before it hits the surface. Needless to say, it takes timing to bring this off delicately. But it's this delicacy combined with accuracy with the various casts which will entice the shy, big fish—truly the big ones—to take your offering.

It takes practice. Start practicing tomorrow on your front lawn or in the basement. Cut the finger tips off an old kid glove and fill them with sand, simulating differently weighted lures. Then set up hoop targets. Hammer away at a target 30 feet away with your battery of casts. Once you have gotten your arm and eye "in" at 30 feet, try a 40-foot target. Then move out to 50 feet. Now combine them, casting at the 30-foot hoop, then the 60, and back to the 50. When you're proficient at these, move the target out to 70, 80 and 90 feet. Although distance will force you to increase the elevation of your release, work to keep a fairly flat trajectory—plus that highly desired silent-dive finish. To save your good line, practice with an old one.

After you've become expert with the sand-filled finger tips, try a real set of lures of different types (removing the hooks, of course), because different lures act differently in the air. When you have

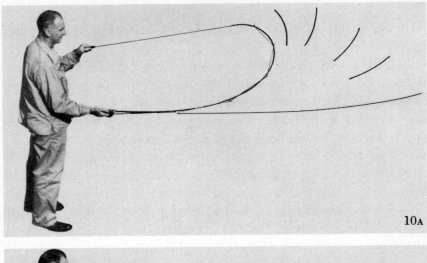

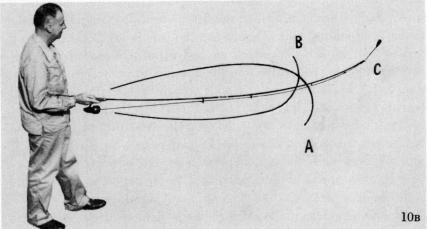

FIGURE 10. *The four trick casts (see also Figure 11) will put a strain on a bamboo rod and may set it. 10A is the catapult shot. Hold the lure with the left hand. Flex the rod tip back. With a bow-and-arrow release, shoot the lure through the opening in the brush. Time your release for the instant before the lure gets byond the rod tip. The wave flip cast (10B) is difficult and requires a fairly short rod—not over 7 feet. It can be your most productive cast in brush-lined water. Poke the rod through the bushes. Hold it in a horizontal plane. Point the rod at the target. With the lure close to the tip, cock the rod sharply down, then up, back down, and make a half-inch forward stab as you release. Although the butt of your rod remains almost stationary, the tip will make a 3-to-5 foot arc—the greater the arc, the better your distance. Released at exactly the right instant, your lure will sail out 50 to 70 feet.*

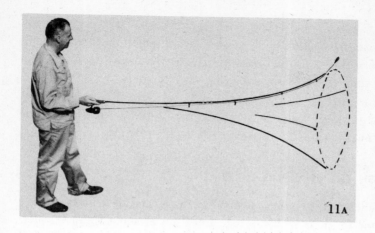

11A

11B

FIGURE 11. *The spin-the-circle cast (11A) drops your lure into difficult, off-to-the-side spots. With the rod tip pointing slightly downward, twirl the lure with the tip as you would a sling. When momentum is gained, let the lure go. Like all close-in shots, this spin-the-circle can be deadly, when mastered, because it will let you get into the seldom-fished spots where big fish rest. By reversing the spin, you can cast the lure backhand.*

Use the down-in-the-front job (11B) when standing on an abrupt bank with brush to both sides and above you. Lower the tip of the rod below your foot level. With the lure hanging from 24 to 30 inches, start swinging the lure in and out and then let 'er go with an up-and-out flip. When standing on a bridge, you can use this cast either upstream or downstream in hard-to-get-to places.

mastered these, try casting them from a sitting position, then a kneeling one, then while standing on the chair. Finally, work with obstructions behind and around you, using the "trick" shots.

With this practice behind you, you'll be agreeably surprised at how productive your next season's fishing will be—providing, of course, you next master the retrieve.

HOW TO FISH THE SPINNING LURES

After you've learned to practice-cast accurately and delicately, you're ready to come to grips with the fish. Let's get at some water.

Test your lure first to determine its best operating speed. Fished faster or slower than its designer intended, it will not produce as well.

For a minute, forget about taking fish. Merely cast and retrieve to get the feel of your lure. As you retrieve, keep your rod tip fairly well down. This produces less wear on your tip top and gossamer line while permitting you to strike the fish more quickly. Now, pretend a fish has hit you. Strike, man, strike! The slip-drag clutch, fortunately, will cancel your overstrike—but even so, don't come back too far. Better than rearing back, strike with a vigorous side strike. If you strike upward, the rod unfortunately goes into a reverse action first and thus gives the fish slack before picking up tension. And don't be so hard on that strike—the hook needs to be moved only a quarter of an inch to set it beyond the barb. Too hard a strike frequently pulls the hook through the tiny ligament by which the fish is held.

Cast again. In retrieving, the important thing is to make the lure act natural. A gob of worms on a big hook even though fished through the most productive bottom-water may fail where a single wriggling worm, impaled lightly on a small sharp hook and drifted through the same pool without tension, will be something which the greedy old bruiser simply cannot deny. Or should you be using an artificial minnow, make it appear that he has been wounded and is struggling, occasionally turning, while the current sweeps him downstream, near the bottom. Even the most jaded lunker will be deceived occasionally into taking a vicious swipe at it.

To get your lure to act naturally, you have several choices: You can open the pick-up finger and let the line run off without interruption; you can manipulate your rod tip, working it up and down, or sideways; or you can give slack and apply tension as your line runs out. Besides these, you can also enlist the help of the current and that's important.

There's more to this natural presentation of imitation minnow than meets the eye. Let's analyze it. Before the angler can fish a minnow properly, he should know the approximate speed of minnows. While growing, a fingerling increases his speed about a mile per hour per inch's length until he is 5 inches long. Thus a 2½-incher can swim about 2½ miles an hour in currentless water, or about 40 feet in 10 seconds. In most streams, the main body of water flows faster than that. How then, can the minnow exist in this fast water? He doesn't. He avoids it. Every stream has quiet, slow areas—particularly near the bottom, behind boulders, in the shallows, or among water weeds as you'll see in Chapter III, "Reading a Stream." Why then should an angler waste most of his time working an imitation streamer fly through four-mile-an-hour water where a true-to-life minnow simply cannot exist, as any dull fish would know? And yet, just about 75 per cent of all stream fishing is done in exactly such unproductive water. The remedy is simple, too. Just let the lure sink down below the swift water and into the quiet bottom water where it can travel at a minnow's true rate of speed, around 2½ miles an hour. And thereby get down, too, to the big-fish, food-on-the-table level of angling. Those anglers who do are deadly.

Let's watch a couple of anglers—Jim and Paul—fish a pool. Both are using the same lure. They can cast equally well. Yet, in fishing our boulder-strewn pool carefully, Jim takes nothing. After resting the pool fifteen minutes, Paul casts to the same spots, apparently, but watch this. When his lure sweeps around the current on the shady side of the first large boulder (get that, the *shady* side which fish prefer in bright sunlight), he raises his rod tip slightly and pays out line so that his lure sinks close to the bottom. Outwardly, it looks much the same as Jim's fishing. But yet, Paul's flashing lure follows the contour of the bottom, working more naturally. At times his lure flutters, then speeds up, and again almost stops in front of the next boulder where he holds it momentarily before letting it sweep on down the stream, threading through a half-dozen boulders and slipping into quiet pocket water behind each one.

Suddenly, Paul strikes. His rod tip snaps down. He's fast to a big fish.

To a top-water reader, Jim and Paul seemed to fish the same water. Actually, they fished two entirely different streams: Jim took the top part which seldom contains fish; Paul took the bottom. Jim covered the pool, Paul fished it—working his lure smack down into the big-fish level. And yet, notice this, too: Paul made perhaps only half as many casts as Jim, but yet, because he fished his lure more slowly, it took him just as much time.

That points up another common fault. Jim, like most anglers, persisted in fishing his lure much too fast. The angler who works his lures slowly, ever so slowly, so as to present a slow-motion imitation of the bait his lure represents, usually collects more strikes from the big fish who like to have their lures move slow and easy, apparently in keeping with their dignified station in life. To do this, consciously, slow down. Slow way down! Now, even s l o w e r ! That's it.

In fishing live bait, it seems even more important than in lure fishing to let the bait bump along the bottom, teasingly, and drift it in and out of the eddies, in front of and behind boulders, and along the bottom of the holding areas in mid-channel. Certainly, you'll foul-hook occasionally but that must be expected in the big-fish league of which you are now a member, in good standing. Show me the man who doesn't get foul-hooked and I'll show you a man who habitually returns with a light creel.

Without question, the spin man has the ideal gear to get down to big-fish level; his threadline sinks quickly behind his weighted lure, and once below the surface it offers little resistance to the water, as lure and line sweep down under the fast tunnel of water where most big fish are.

The current and depth of a stream pretty well dictate how to fish moving water. When the cast is made across and beyond the swift current into the slow water, a few turns of the reel handle may be necessary to keep the lure in motion and off the bottom until the sweep of the current catches it. When it does, a very strong current may yank your lure across and sweep it downstream in a most unnatural manner and well above the bottom. What to do? As soon as the swift water hits the lure, strip off a yard or two of line, quickly, so that the lure can drop through the swift water to the bottom and work there along the much slower productive water. The amount of line you will feed out will depend upon the tug of the stream, the depth of the water, the weight of your line and the way your particular lure acts.

The feel of your lure is perhaps your best tip-off. When it hangs in the current, a throbbing can usually be felt. With practice, the throbbing will telegraph the right tempo of your retrieve.

Should there be little current in the water and should the pool be deep, change pace constantly. After the cast, let the lure sink a few feet, then reel, sinking and reeling in different lengths and different levels. This way, you will induce vertical action along with horizontal, which may be effective. But occasionally, make a steady retrieve, too. That's fishing.

When drifting live bait, always try for a natural action, and in faster water keep the bait near the bottom of the main channel. Usually, it's best to keep the pick-up arm off and hold the line by touching the spool with your index finger. Should the bait pull steady and tend to come off the bottom, pay out line. If necessary, wave your rod tip across gently to speed extra line through the guides. But don't get out too much line, either. Maintain a sufficient tension to be ready to hook the fish without a lot of slack intervening. Your sensitive rod tip will tell you when the bait drags on the bottom. Stop feeding more line, and lift the rod slightly.

Whenever your bait seems to touch bottom, be suspicious. Your bottom may have fins on it. When in doubt, retrieve carefully, so that the bait's motion retains its naturalness. With a fish on, you'll feel a throb. Then, strike! But should you have touched bottom, and not snagged, your gentle lifting may have activated your bait just enough to provoke a fish into snatching it up. Or if a fish does not take it, your gentle action has not wigwagged an alarm through Fish Haven.

You'll simply prolong your drift downstream and perhaps take a fish down there.

Fishing a lake successfully with its undefined bottom, picking out the best food and resting areas, is much more difficult at first than fishing a stream where most of the bottom is in sight. "Reading a Lake," Chapter III, will explain this more fully. But lake fishing can be rewarding—fish tend to be heavier there.

Once again, study to make your lure act natural. What the lake fish eats and how he captures it should establish the basis of your retrieve. As you know, most big fish like nothing better to eat than little fish—and a good share of their diet consists of exactly that, small fish, plus frogs, and nymphs, and anything good that falls in the water.

Study a frog in the water. Does he swim steadily as so many anglers' retrieves might indicate? Not at all. He pauses frequently in his swimming, resting motionless on the water, legs outspread in a most undignified manner, then he kicks ahead in short jerks for a few feet and rests again, motionless, with only his eye stems protruding from the water. 'With a mouse, it's different. It swims slowly and steadily. A crawfish darts from one to three feet, pauses, then darts again. Isn't it obvious? To fish these fish-food imitators, the frog lure should be jerked a foot or so and then allowed to rest motionless on the water for several seconds; the mouse should be kept moving, slowly but regularly; the crawfish should be darted in an angular manner—action imparted by switching the rod tip from side to side during the retrieve; the minnow should twist, dart and wobble, or be retrieved steadily, or with pauses; or, as the fish follows it, speeded up slightly as though it's attempting a frantic escape. Futile, we hope.

Instead of always casting the frog lure toward the shore, occasionally turn about and cast it into deeper water and retrieve it to simulate a frog swimming toward shore.

When fishing from a boat, cast your lure occasionally on the bank itself, particularly if it seems to have an undercut big enough to harbor a fish, and then hop it off—rest, reel; pause, reel—all of which adds to the interest of the lure and its appeal to the fish which may be ogling it. With a surface plug, the retrieve has not yet been invented which is slow enough. If you'll take five minutes to retrieve each cast, you'll fill your limit in large fish in just half the time.

In making your casts from shore, let your lure sink clear to the bottom. Retrieve it in short pulls, lifting it off the bottom by raising your rod each time. Keep this up until you can see your lure. If no fish is following, don't waste time. Reel in quickly for another cast. In the last analysis, the proportion of time your lure is in productive areas determines the proportion of action you have. However, when your lure lifts from the water let it dangle an instant or two to untwist your line.

If a lake has a cliff, there'll usually be a ledge slightly below the water's surface with broken boulders in the deep water below that. Retrieve the lure, letting it flutter and sink occasionally, along the entire length of the ledge at various levels, including the bottom level among the rocks, and once, again, with varying retrieves.

Most salt-water spinning is done along beaches, in bays, inlets, up tidal rivers or in flats. Because of tide and wave action, salt-water fishing is largely a combination of both lake and stream spin fishing. For best results, cast into eddies and retrieve just as you would in a stream. When fishing an estuary with steep cliff-like banks, fish it much as you would a lake, retrieving along the ledges at varying levels. Where to look for salt-water fish will be amply covered in Chapter III, "Reading Salt Water."

Perhaps because most salt-water game fish grow faster and are more voracious and usually feed on faster-moving food, they prefer lures which are retrieved faster than those in sweet water. That goes for trolling, too. Many won't more than glance at a slowly retrieved lure. However, with a fresh bait, cast it well out and let it stay put until the cruising fish comes along and takes it. A slight tension on the bait will enable you to strike the fish when he takes it—but, here again, there are exceptions. In striper water, for example, it is usually best to let the fish pick it up and move about 10 feet with it and then strike because stripers have the disconcerting habit of mouthing their bait for some time before really taking it for keeps.

As he spins, the angler will of course devise retrieves of his own. That is how I worked out one of my killers. I was bait casting on a

lake, and in trying for extra distance, got a back lash. The lure settled
to the deep bottom, almost beneath the boat. In picking out the back
lash, I must have jiggled the lure because, suddenly, I got a hard
strike and unprepared, missed. I would have thought little about it
beyond the cussed perversity of bass if I hadn't gotten another strike
as I reeled up the lure. This time I set the hook and was fast to the
one and only good-sized fish of the day. It didn't dawn on me until
that evening that I should have tried that vertical retrieve again. Since
then, I do it quite frequently and the spinman will find it a mighty
good addition to his repertoire of retrieves. When over a weed bed,
let your lure drop straight down. Rest it a couple of seconds, and
then reel it straight up. Next time, jig it up, keeping it wobbling
and weaving. Sure you'll get hung up occasionally—but just as often
you'll hang up into an animated hunk of flesh.

  Now why should a halfway intelligent fish fall for a straight-up
retrieve? Ever see a minnow come to the surface from a weed bed?
Or a nymph? And so, you see, it's a natural action.

  I've purposely saved trolling—also a method of lure retrieving
in sweet and salt water—for the last. Exceedingly exciting times can
be had by trolling with a light spinning outfit in slow-moving river,
lake or salt water. Also, it can be a good way of discovering where
the fish are—by working different levels. Streamer flies can be particularly good. The spinning reel is ideal for this. Simply set the
anti-reverse and hang on. Run one streamer fly out in the wash of
the boat, up fairly close, not more than 30 feet away. Better mark
your line with a red thread. The water action and the flash of your
propeller seem to attract the big ones. Hint: Why not keep your prop
blades polished? Then have your partner work a second fly just off
the wake, 40 feet behind the boat. Attracted by the wake, the fish
may follow the first fly some distance. Then, turning from that, he
often sees the second fly, and man, how his strike will make your
rod jump!

  If steady trolling does not deliver, try variations. Let out more
line and troll more slowly; this will put the fly deeper. Or jerk it
spasmodically, every 15 or 20 seconds, bringing it in with sharp
18-inch jabs, and then let it go again to give your fly a sort of helpless,

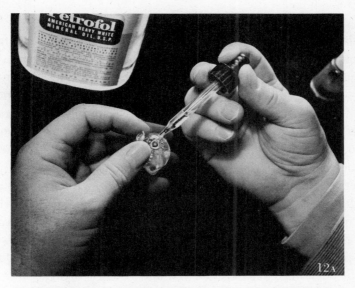

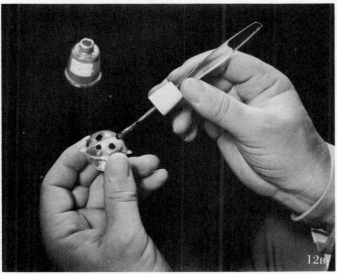

FIGURE 12. *Fill your bubbles at home. Using mineral oil (12A) prevents evaporation and loss of weight. The cork tends to pop out upon hitting the water—hence, after you have eye-droppered the desired amount, seal the plug with fingernail polish (12B). To increase visibility daub some spots with red or yellow fingernail polish—the latter, of course, can be seen farther.*

struggling action. This retrieve worked extremely well one fall off Qualicum Beach, Vancouver Island, when I was skipping my Cohoe streamer fly across the top of the choppy water and hanging into silvers running anywhere from 5 to 10 pounds. What wonderful action that was on my 2½-ounce Winston hollow-fluted bamboo rod.

When the sun climbs, the salmon often seem to go deeper, perhaps to avoid the brightness. When they do this, it is highly profitable to go down too with your trolled lure—perhaps even down to 50 or 75 feet. To get down there with your light trolling outfit, suspend an independently weighted line from the side of the boat. Have a clothespin attached near the heavy lead weight. Then run from 30 to 50 feet of your fine spinning line beyond the clothespin's jaws. When the salmon strikes your lure, he'll automatically jerk your line free and then all that's between you and your cavorting fish is a fine line and a light rod. That's sport, raised to the third power.

SPINNING WITH A BUBBLE

This may be hard to believe. As many an angler knows, it can take up to 20 years of hard fishing to become a truly accomplished dry-fly angler. Yet, by using a weighted plastic bubble, it is possible for the spinman, within twenty minutes—that's right, minutes not years—to cast a tiny No. 16 dry fly 75 feet with a 4-ounce rod into trouty water and then do what no dry-fly man ever could do—hop-skip that dry fly on the water and make it resemble an insect laying eggs. With what result? You guessed it. That egg-laying action, far out in comparatively unfished water, will even drive big trout nutty. And what a show it is to see adult fish, who ought to know better, bounce out of the water, time and again, in their frenzy to hit your hopped-up fly. Do you wonder why even the most casehardened dry-fly purists are taking to spinning with a light rod and bubble?

When the bubble is properly fished—up to now it hasn't been 99 per cent of the time—not only can the dry fly be deadly but also the nymph, wet-fly, streamer, single salmon egg or hellgrammite.

Unfortunately, most bubbles are incorrectly designed. The manufacturers' only thought, apparently, has been to provide the spinman

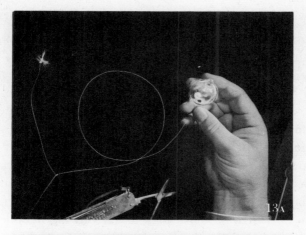

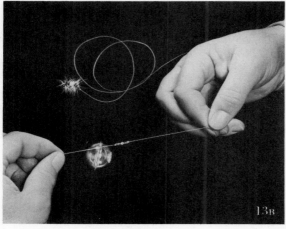

FIGURE 13. *Six feet from the end of your 3-pound test platyl line (you'll come down to 2) tie a blood knot, leaving one eight-inch end (13A). To this knot attach your well-hackled dry fly with a Turle knot. Then, to the end of the line attach your quarter-filled plastic bubble, threading the line through both holes and coming back once, for strength's sake, because those earholes aren't very strong, and tie a jam knot. To get a natural deep-running float with your lure, thread the line through the tiny earhole but do not tie it—and your line will run free. This will permit you to set the hook without having to move the bubble. To prevent the free-running bubble from working out to the lure, attach a swivel (13B) to the casting line, and fasten the leader to that with bait or hook. To keep the bubble from walking up the line, tie a string, wherever desired, with a series of half hitches, which will permit the knot to slip through the guides while casting.*

with enough weight to carry out his weightless lures. However, with improvisation, the angler can remedy most shortcomings.

To begin, most bubbles are difficult to fill on the streamside unless you fill your mouth with water and spew it into the tiny hole. An easier way is to fill them at home with an eye dropper. To get your line to slide easily through the bubble's tiny earholes you may have to enlarge one of them, but slightly. The best idea, of course, is to make up a set of variously weighted bubbles. Sometimes when the wind is behind the caster, he will want only an extremely light bubble; when casting into the wind, a heavier one; and then there are times when he will want more than to half-fill the bubble so that it will sink. And for swift water, he may even want an additional 1 to 3 BB shots in the bubble. See Figure 12 for preparation of bubble.

Let's try that hop-skipping dry-fly cast first. It's easier than wet fly or nymph. To make a dry-fly skitter insectlike, see Figure 13.

With a side swing, cast your dry fly above the trouty area where fast water meets slow. As with a lure, tighten up on it slightly in mid-air to extract the weighted bubble's momentum and let it alight on the water gently. Keep your rod tip up to hold most of your gossamer line out of the water. As the fly rides, twitch the rod tip and the dangling fly will pepper the water. And if you've cast so that the fly will hop-skip-and-jump through the "hot spot" and trout are on the peck, you're in for some trout-happy action.

To float properly, the dry fly must be dressed with stiff hackles and waterproofed. I prefer a Gantron-bodied, hollow deer-hair wing Caddis, in the John Kolzer pattern, but small. (John lives on the McKenzie, Blue River, Oregon. He's the kind of tyer who usually adds a note of explanation with his flies.) After taking a fish, swish the dry fly through the water to rid it of blood and slime, squeeze out the superfluous moisture with a sheet of absorbent Kleenex, then blow on the fly and dunk it in a waterproofing compound. (I use a home-made preparation: one part of solid Mucilin to three parts carbon tetrachloride, better known as cleaning fluid.) Knock off the excess, blow on the fly from behind to fluff it, and get along with your wonderful fishing. Should the trout ignore one dry-fly pattern, slip on another for size and silhouette. If that doesn't produce, why not try a nymph

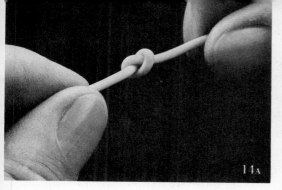

14A

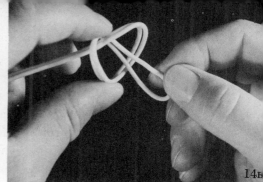

14B

14C

FIGURE 14. *This pesky overhand knot (14A) so easily picked up when casting, will reduce your 4-pound test line to 1 pound! Best to do: Break the line and retie! Leaders seldom part —it's your knots that give first! Many anglers are content to use a simple double overhand knot to make a loop (14B). This reduces your 4-pound test line to 2 pounds. Don't use it. This (14C) is a wonderful new knot and produces the nearest thing to a 100-per-cent loop knot that there is! (It tests 99 per cent.) Make about 15 turns with your right fingers, rotating them around the left hand. Roll the loop up tighter with the forefinger and thumb of your left hand while spreading the loop with your two right-hand fingers which are within the loop (14D). This allows the end to twist back on the loop. Then make a half hitch on the near side of the loop (14E); and make another half hitch on the far side (14F). Then, to finish off the knot, slip the front of the knot back ever so slightly to prevent shearing the knot at the front. Pull up, and trim the end. Test it, and you'll find the line usually parts before the knot breaks. Could anything be better?* Knot pictures used by permission of Outdoor Life.

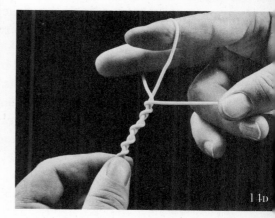

14D

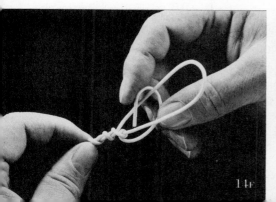

14F

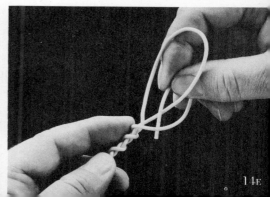

14E

fished an inch beneath the surface so it bulges the water? If they still don't cotton up to it at this level, drop it 18 inches and raise the rod gently to make the nymph appear to be struggling upward in the water. If this doesn't produce and the stream has a fairly even floor, drop a long leader to take the nymph down to the bottom, allowing extra line for it to trail because bottom water travels slower than top water as you'll see in "Reading a Stream," Chapter III. For this nymphing Dan Bailey's Devil's Scratcher often produces. (Address Dan Bailey's Sport Shop, Livingston, Montana. And if you want to see the outlines of more than a hundred big trout taken on flies—every fish is from four to seventeen pounds—drop into his shop and drool!) In this fishing, the bubble acts both as floater and bobber. When the fish strikes, the bubble will act unnaturally, perhaps even go under. To connect with the fish, strike immediately.

With an uneven floor—the usual condition—it's better to change the method of using your float. Now, thread the line through the ear-hole of the bubble and let the line run *free,* not anchored to your bubble. This will permit your bait to follow the contour of the bottom where big fish spend just about nine-tenths of their waking time getting about nine-tenths of their food.

The free line has this further advantage—and a very important one: the fish strike against the rod—not against the bubble—which allows you to strike the fish before he can spit it out. Also, you have a better chance of hooking the fish because you do not have to move the bubble before the hook can be set. It comes under the heading of keeping in constant communication with the business end of your gear without having the information held up or sidetracked permanently by the intervening bubble.

Although some fish have made my rod jump in taking Dan's juicy-looking Devil's Scratcher, particularly when it bulged the surface, usually the strikes are so imperceptible that they might well pass unnoticed by the beginner and he will go fishless while the experienced man, alongside, will fill his creel with big ones. It is always good operational procedure to lift the rod a little *every time* the bubble acts the least bit unnatural. If no fish is engaged, no damage has been done. The float has not been moved from its natural

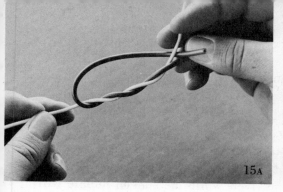

15A

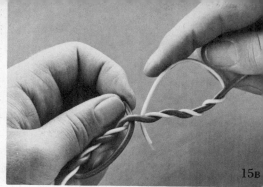

15B

FIGURE 15. *The blood knot is the strongest knot for linking two pieces of almost the same diameter line. It tests 86 per cent. Twist one end of the joining lengths 3½ times and turn the bend back (15A). Repeat the same process (15B), with the other end and tuck it in the end from the opposite side. Snug them up—if you use nylon, do it steadily; if you use gut, give it a slight jerk to set the knot. This knot also serves when you're fishing among weeds or barnacles or want to use a heavier lure— you'll want to add a slightly heavier leader. Use it also to knot an extra fine gut or nylon tippet. This timeless knot (15C) is used by many fishermen for linking two pieces of line or leader. It tests at least 29 per cent weaker than the blood knot and has the tendency to slip with nylon or platyl. Why use it? This is a dropper knot (15D). Twist your line, drop the tongue through the gap and snub up the knot. Many anglers, including the writer, prefer the blood knot to a dropper (it tests 86 per cent), simply letting one of the overlapping ends dangle (see 15B). This loop knot (15F) is extremely easy to make and will strengthen the single loop knot (shown in Figure 14B). Merely push the loop through a second time (15E). Pull up and you have the finished product (15F).* Knot pictures used by permission of Outdoor Life.

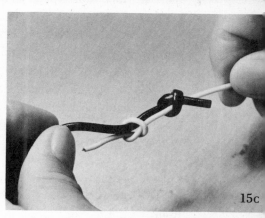

15C

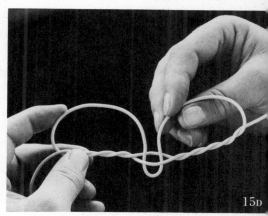

15D

15F

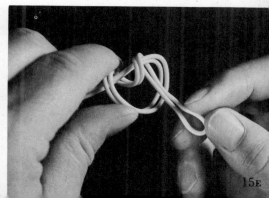

15E

drift, thanks to the slip-attachment, and you can continue to fish out the cast uninterrupted.

Even with a weighted bubble, in swift water, it may be necessary to use a light split-shot sinker near the bait or the fly to keep them at the bottom. You will find that this combination more than any other will put your lure close to the bottom where it will adjust its speed to the natural bottom-speed of the river, while the sunken bubble will keep the lure in mid-channel.

When the bubble comes to the end of the float, count to ten before you begin your retrieve, slowly, unevenly, taking at least twenty seconds to bring it up within rod's length.

The weighted float can be fished upstream, downstream or across. Some accomplished spinmen fish it mostly upstream. This calls for short casts. As the lure comes downstream, these anglers must maintain a light tension and yet not so tight but what the lure can act natural. It's exacting fishing.

It is much easier to fish across stream and let your nymph, bait or wet fly work down with the surface-riding bubble; and it can be highly productive, too, as it allows the spinman to fish water which the conventional angler usually cannot reach, thus capitalizing upon the superiority of the spinning tackle.

In fishing with a bubble downstream, some extremely long floats can be extracted. As the float rides downstream, open the pick-up and allow the threadline to pay out without drag. Use your index finger to control the release of the line, snubbing it up promptly should a strike be telegraphed through from the front.

Occasionally a big fish with an inordinately large curiosity bump will rise to size up the bubble. I'm the accommodating kind. If, in tying my bubble to the line, I have left a 4-inch end dangling from the jam knot I can supply him with something worth taking—such as a Devil's Scratcher. In big bass water, particularly, you'll be agreeably amazed at how often this extra hook near the bubble will take a big fish. It comes under the heading of exploiting your tackle to the utmost. Some states think this is taking unfair advantage of the fish—and prohibit the use of more than one hook. Check, before you use it.

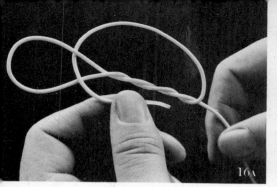

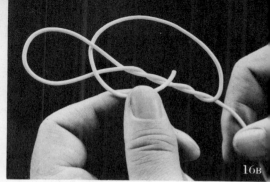

16A

16B

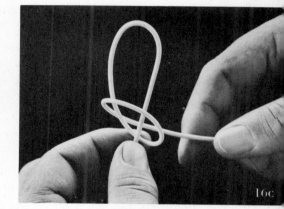

16C

FIGURE 16. *This is the jam knot (16A), used for tying on the lure. It normally tests about 87 per cent; yet if the end is tucked through the loop (16B), it picks up almost 10 per cent extra strength and in use will slip less readily—a very important factor with synthetic lines and leaders. It is especially good when using a heavy hook when wet-fly and nymph fishing for steelhead.*

The succeeding knots are intended primarily for the angler who insists upon taking his fly line and light-fly reel with him for dry-fly fishing with his spinning rod. This is the perfection loop knot used on the butt end of your leader for fly fishing. It tests 88 per cent. Make two loops as in (16C); then add a third loop between these two (16D). Reach through the first loop and get the more distant loop (16E), and pull it through and snug it up (16F), and you have a beautiful, serviceable knot. Knot pictures used by permission of Outdoor Life.

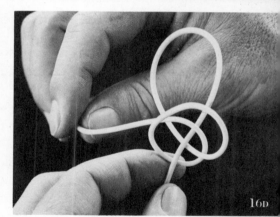

16D

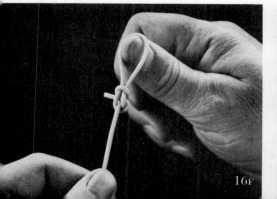

16F

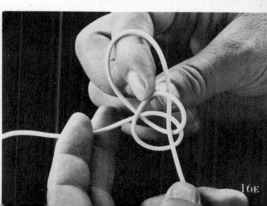

16E

BEST KNOTS FOR SPINNING

The biggest single improvement any spin caster can make is to spend just one evening mastering five knots—eight if he wishes to fly fish. By using the correct knot, even the seasoned angler may increase his take-home catch by 25 per cent and improve his chances of landing his trophy fish by 100 per cent!

Besides, with his gossamer nylon and platyl lines, it is absolutely essential that the spinman discard his old knots and learn these new ones because the old usually let go under tension. With big fish on, that's heartbreaking. I have tested the knots in Figures 14 to 17 with a Scott thread-testing machine.

New knots will save you money: you'll not lose as many lures and you'll not leave so many in big fish—the kind of fish you want to bring home for the wall.

Convinced? All right, but first a general observation: To avoid shearing, bring your nylon or platyl knots up slowly and finish-pull them tightly. But if you insist on dry-fly fishing and using gut tippets, as I do, bring your knot up with a jerk to set it. (I'm about to change my mind, though, after seeing the brand new Platyl knotless tapered leaders put out by Charles Garcia & Co., 53 Park Place, New York City 7. A 6x tippet tests approximately 3 lbs!)

For the strongest knot possible to tie line to reel, see the loop knot, Figure 14C. For splicing two lines, see the blood knot (Figure 15A).

In tying on the lure, the angler must decide whether he wants the strongest possible knot—and jeopardize losing a lot of line with his lure—or a knot which is a little weaker than the line, so that when he has to pull his foul-hooked lure free it will part at the knot which links line to lure. For good solutions, see the double loop knot (Figure 14B) and the jam knot (Figure 16A).

If the spinman is a reconstructed dry-fly man, he'll want to take his fly reel along, and will need the best knots:

The loop knot, for tying tapered leader to tapered line (Figure 14C).

The figure-eight knot, for attaching the line to leader (Figure 17A).

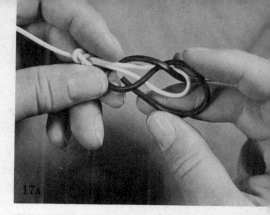

17A

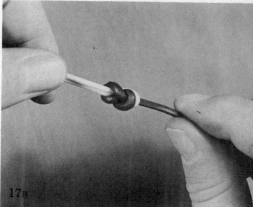

17B

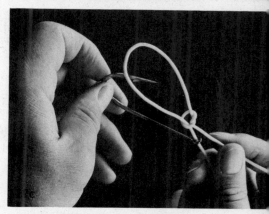

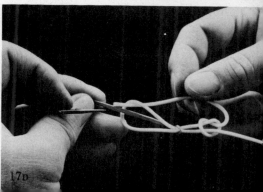

17D

FIGURE 17. *This figure-eight knot (17A) is intended to attach the tapered fly line to the butt loop of the leader. Run the line through the loop and tuck the end under and then bring the line over and tuck it in from behind. Trim the end up close and you have a knot (17B), which will not slip and it leaves no bothersome end exposed on which to foul up the point of your leader. (17C) This is the Turle knot, not turtle! It's good for attaching fly to leader. Pull the guy tippet through the hook's eye. Make a loop and slip it over the barb of the hook. Its breaking strength is 80 per cent. For nylon, put the end through the small knot twice to prevent the knot from slipping. This double-eye knot (17D) raises the breaking point of the popular Turle about 7 per cent. Put the tippet through the eye, around the back of the shank and up through the eye again. Make a slip knot and tuck the end back through the loop. Tighten up. That's it. Now you're knot-sure for fishing.* Pictures used by permission of Outdoor Life.

The Turle knot and the double-eye knot, for attaching fly to leader (Figures 17C and 17D).

With a working knowledge of these knots, the angler will derive two benefits: first, he will increase the maximum strength of his spinning line from 5 to 75 per cent; and, second, because of this bonus strength, he can go down to an even lighter weight test line, and this invariably spells more and bigger fish action in water where the big ones come shy.

III. FISH AND WATER

READING A STREAM

What you are going to read now should put big fish on your rod because it will tell you where big fish hang out in moving water.

First, the angler must realize that fish—even the fleet-finned rainbow trout—avoid water which exceeds 2½ miles an hour. They are more at home in mile-an-hour water, and if it is slower so much the better. That's for resting. For feeding, they also like slow water but usually near fast water where the current will carry food to them on a platter. Finally, they want to be near a spot where they can hide. That's for safety.

But in a swift stream, where can they ever find slow, restful water?

Speed of water is most deceptive. For example, cascading white water may be much slower than gliding smooth-topped water. Where there's white water there's been dissipation of energy. Furthermore, water flows at different speeds from top to bottom and that's what affects the angler most.

With this variation of speeds from bottom to top, how does the hydraulic expert measure true speed? The answer is, he's worked out a formula. He takes two readings, one one-fifth of the way from the top and the other one-fifth of the way from the bottom. The two, averaged, come very close to giving the exact answer.

To observe the variations, let's take an easy piece of water to read such as a U-shaped canal. Most of us have already surmised that in such a canal, the water has a slight drag on the bottom and sides. Slight? My eye! It's fully two-thirds slower! And due to surface tension, the top layer also has a drag. Actually, the fastest water in a canal travels in a tunnel-like tube, pretty well toward the top half of the canal, and it slows up decidedly toward both bottom and sides. For example, when it flows at 3 miles an hour in this center tunnel-like tube, it often flows less than $\frac{1}{2}$ mile an hour near the bottom.

But a complex stream, of course, is vastly different. It has an uneven floor, varying widths, and a rock-strewn bottom. And these things are of extreme importance to your fish because they tend to form slow-water areas. Water flowing around a rock, for example, will tend to assume a streamlined shape, leaving a dead-water envelope around the rock not unlike the appearance of a cross cut of an airplane wing, or a teardrop. That is why, even in fast water, insects can cling to a rock and algae can grow on it. This dead-water envelope means that there is a quiet-water area ahead of the boulder, a narrow one along either side, and a larger tail-like one in back of the rock. Multiply this rock by thousands—for every rock on the stream's floor—and the angler will begin to understand part of the reason for the uneven flow of water in any stream and for the vast numberless quiet-water pockets that exist even in the swiftest of streams. Besides boulders, of course, there are ledges, uneven bottoms and sides, undercut banks, roots, grasses and submerged logs.

Now where does the fish live and travel? Exactly as you'd suspect, he rests in front of and behind the boulders, ledges and undercut banks, and when uninterrupted by a tactless angler, he usually travels in the slowest-moving water, which occurs toward the bottom and sides. Because he is streamlined, he always heads up-current. In this respect, it is most interesting to see how the salmon and steelhead pick their way in their upstream migration. In seeking the soft spots, they unerringly zigzag up the stream bed, hugging the bottom, and with their bellies and fins brush the silt and algae off rocks, leaving behind a clearly defined highway—as one fish follows the other along the path of least resistance.

Enough for the resting spots and the highways. For our devices,

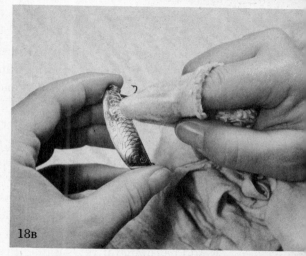

18A

FIGURE 18.   *Lures carry easily in several compartmented plastic boxes—only the compartments are usually too small for many of the lures. In the box (18A), there were originally eight compartments. It was a simple matter to break out some of the compartments, as is being done with the thumb.*

(18B) One secret of bringing home heavy fish is to keep your lures bright. Shine them up before you leave home—and don't touch the surface with your fingers; this leaves finger marks which soon tarnish and get dull. Polish them while fishing, too. (18C) It is possible to troll for big fish, way down deep, with a light spinning outfit. Simply lower an independently hung weight to which a clothespin is attached. Then, at some distance— 40 feet or so—troll your lure with your line running through the jaws of the clothespin. When the fish strikes, he will free your line. Raise the weight and fight the fish, unencumbered, with a light outfit. Man, that's sport supreme!

18B

18C

the more important question is: "Where are their feeding stations?"

Usually, resting and feeding stations are the same, or very near together. As to be expected, the fish prefer to stay in slow water but near enough to fast water so that the current can deposit food at their front door. And there, where fast water meets slow, is where you'll usually find the big fish sitting down to his daily fare.

Sometimes there is a clue—not always—in picking out this "hot spot." In big water, where fast food-bearing water meets slow resting-water, there's usually a triangular area on the surface filled with small jumpy wave water—pointed waves that move up and down and get exactly nowhere. By the very nature of the water's action, these areas are usually near deep gouged-out pools, or near boulders, or near an undercut bank so that the fish has his personal foxhole near by.

To be sure, a skillful surface angler will occasionally extract large fish near the top in swift water—but by the nature of the big fish's food, habits and resting places, lunkers and surface anglers seldom get together.

In the less swift stream water, there will be other food-safety-rest areas. Sometimes they will be along shaded ledges, under roots, and often under overhanging branches which not only provide shade and coolness to the water but also food in the form of bugs, larvae, caterpillars and even mice or an occasional fledgling.

To exploit these "hot spots" demands precision in lure presentation. If that meant only hitting a trout on the nose every time, it would be comparatively simple. Precision with a spinning lure means much more than that. The angler must select his spot to cast to maybe ten, twenty or even thirty feet away, from which his lure will sweep down to the big fish's exact location despite the onrushing current. But even so, the spinman is not to be pitied. After all, he has the ideal gear to work his lure to the bottom where the big fish are—and if the lure's action is attractive, woe to the fish!

READING A LAKE

Instead of talking about it, let's go fishing. It's mid-July, a bright cloudless day, without a breath of air stirring. Warm, too. Not the best weather for fishing, you say? Say, any day's good when you're fishing. But even so, good weather or bad, there's seldom an hour—day or night—on any lake when big fish aren't feeding somewhere.

See that high cliff over there on the south end of the lake with the maidenhair fronds cascading from it? Yup, and listen. There's an ouzel's song. That maidenhair and the bird's song may mean fish. Then, off there to the east, see all those willows? Looks a little boggy from here, doesn't it? Must be some beaver work. Make you a bet that near the other end of the lake you'll find a second boggy area, only it will be choked, full of sunken logs and broken stumps. And now that we've climbed and gotten some elevation, see how the lake narrows and then opens up into a second arm? And there, almost directly across from the cliff, there's a meadow. The land flattens out and just as one might suspect, along the water's edge are bulrushes, In the lazy, warm sunshine, some blue darning needles dip down over the water in their swift flight. Except for them, the lake lies motionless. And fishless? Well, hold on, just a minute.

Before breaking down this big lake to "reading" size, let's make some general observations. First, whether in lake or stream, fish are confronted with two abiding problems: Where do we eat next? and, Where can we be safe? In quiet water, rest isn't a factor except insofar as the fish avoids bright sunlight and warm water.

As for protection that's fairly easy. There are usually snags, sunken logs, boulders which have broken off cliffs, and hiding places among the weed beds.

As for food, that's another matter. When a fish's protective area does not supply it in ample amounts, the fish just naturally has to pick up and go after it. That means he has to make periodic forays to the food-laden shallower water. And this is dangerous. Therefore you may be sure that the wise old fish who has escaped countless predators, including man, will continue to use the utmost caution and as far as possible see that his feeding grounds are close to his hiding area. Every foot less the distance between these two, the longer his life expectancy.

With these commonplace observations behind us, let's get into the boat. But just a second. Let's take a look at the lay of the lake

from our slight elevation. Actually, a contour study can tell us a great
deal about the hidden bottom and the food areas. Shallow flat shore
lines mean shallow flat lakes. Rugged sides invariably mean deep,
steep banks. And a cliff usually breaks off just below the water's
edge, making a narrow ledge and beyond that a steeply-shelving
bottom covered with huge boulders which have broken off the cliff—
ideal hiding places.

How do we know a shelf is there? That's because there is more
weathering on the cliff above the waterline than under. Above, it
meets wind and rain, winter and summer—in winter, ice in tiny
cracks expands and then melts and freezes and expands some more.
In summer, the rock expands with the heat and contracts with the
midnight chill. And so, the wall breaks down.

On the other side, where we saw the meadow, the water is shallow
and warm and it slopes out gently. But yet, not so very far—perhaps
150 feet out—you'll find an abrupt drop-off. Once again, it's the
contour.

Imperceptible as they may seem, definite currents are set up
in every lake which has intakes—whether these be bottom-fed springs
or incoming brooks—because of the differences in densities and tem-
peratures and the flow of water from intake to outlet. Around these
currents, fish set up their day-to-day cycles, which remain pretty
constant within a seasonal cycle.

About those willows we saw, they must be near an inlet of cold
water. As for the outlet, you could bet on those sunken logs being
there because the freshets and the lake's current would have carried
them there where they eventually got waterlogged and sank.

Remember that maidenhair fern on the cliff? That means there's
water dripping and a cold spring underneath. Quite a bit of water,
too, or we wouldn't have heard that ouzel's song. Expect a cool spring
below, where fish will congregate hot afternoons, particularly in mid-
July, because there is plenty of shade there too. The cliff is on the
lake's south side—as though the maidenhair didn't tell us that already.
Makes it a good place to fish in summer but usually a poor place in
spring, when the bottom life is slow and retarded in this cooler area.

Let's row over to that sloping shore, directly across from the cliff. See, just as we expected, it drops off suddenly over a rock ledge. Watch those oarlocks. We've got to approach carefully. In shallows, fish seem to frighten more easily—maybe it's because they are farther from a haven of refuge and keep one eye cocked for poachers. And don't move any more than you have to. Fish spot motion a long way off. But keep right on talking. Conversational noises, unless terribly loud, do not penetrate the water like the sound from an oarlock which seems to be amplified by the boat's bottom. Foot noises are bad too.

We'll spin the shoals first, just in case. Then, fish your lure deeper, bringing it past the deep drop-off ledge. Sometimes this area will "fish" more easily when you move your boat alongside the edge of this ledge and lower your anchor very quietly.

Next let's explore that covelike inlet with the boggy water and the tangle of willows. Such overhung coves usually have weed beds, too, full of bottom food. Look for a small creek entering it, a wonderful food and cool-water carrier. Approach this shallow area carefully—unless you're satisfied with merely seeing a slight telltale cloud of muddy water rising from where a big one skipped out ahead of your approach.

Purposely, I've been saving the narrows for late-afternoon fishing. This is a fine spot to take advantage of moving fish. In foraging up and down a lake shore, fish must congregate, obviously, to pass through such narrows. Mathematically, more cruising fish must be found here per cubic yard than in any other part of the lake. Hence it may be highly profitable for us to anchor the boat and work over what trout, salmon and bass may be going through. Similarly, points of land jutting out into a lake are good congregating areas.

That tried, let's fish the weed beds. It was downright careless of us not to have tried them sooner. Remember those darning needles? That meant that a hatch was on. It meant, too, that big fish were below, gorging on their helpless cousins who never had a ghost of a chance to make the surface with these lunkers behind them. A vertically retrieved nymph might have taken those lunkers a little earlier.

A more steady hatch, though, ought to be coming off those sunken logs where the lake drains. Around such logs, aquatic life usually abounds, and throughout a warm day, stone, caddis or dragonfly nymphs will continue to hatch freely.

Wind, sun and season have very definite bearing on still-water fishing. During bright sunlight, fish tend to get down deeper and away from the sun's glare, and whenever possible you'll find the fish on the shady side of the street. That's when to look for them under overhanging tree branches, along ledges, or deep down among the weed beds. Should the wind ruffle the water, that will lower the amount of brightness which enters the water and drive more life saving, refreshing oxygen into the water besides depositing thousands of mosquitoes, grasshoppers, and an occasional fledgling who failed his solo flight.

With the approach of hot weather, as the lake grows warmer, most game fish will abandon their shore-line feeding during the day and seek the cool comfort of deeper, shaded water. But how deep?

As the lake warms, its water levels off into three distinct layers. The top contains the warm water which is lighter and has less density. This layer's depth will depend upon the lake's size and the amount of hot weather. The lowest layer, on the contrary, is deep, uniformly cold, and because wave water cannot reach it, this layer has the least oxygen. Unless there is ample plant life to release oxygen and absorb carbon dioxide, it is positively deadly to fish.

Successful spin fishing in summer usually lies between these two extremes—in the middle layer. Here the temperature is more comfortable, the oxygen supply is adequate, and usually there are mouthfuls of small fry. This optimum layer, called the *thermocline*, may start at ten feet below the surface in small lakes or at fifty feet or more in extremely large, deep bodies of water. Since it is the thinnest of the three layers, don't depend upon luck to locate it. Trolling at different depths until you've hit the fish-bearing stratum is too time-consuming. Much simpler is to lower a minimum-maximum thermometer and take readings at 5-foot intervals. Soon you will have charted the three layers with surprising accuracy because the thermocline changes its temperature abruptly, say, from 50 degrees to 70 degrees Fahrenheit in 10 feet while the other two change temperature very slowly.

However, despite the thermocline, the greedy old bass haven't forgotten the location of their shore-line breadbox and they will make excursions to it occasionally by day but usually by night. As a result, it is a good place to start the day's spinning operations, but make it early, while the water is coolest and the wise old bass haven't been frightened by the daily horde of tackle-rattlers.

Fortified with this lake information, the spinman should now be able to read lake water with much more understanding—and even though a large lake may seem baffling at first sight, with a little experience he'll be able to read it as he rows and get that spine-tingling response that goes with swinging into heavy lake fish on a light rod and gossamer threadline.

READING SALT WATER

The immensity of the sea usually overwhelms the beginning salt-water spinman until he becomes observant, after which he suddenly finds that salt water "reads" easy. Everywhere about him are count-less clues telling him where fish can be caught. By watching a seal catch fish one afternoon, I found a most productive striper fishing hole behind a sheltered reef. Another time, I found a clam bed which had been exposed after a storm. It was just about as obvious as find-ing a table set for dinner. Next high tide, sure enough, I took my red fish. Locate the ocean fish's food supply and he's yours for the casting.

Three things determine the movement of fish seeking food along the coast where the surf caster operates: wind, tide and current. Of these, tide is most important. It determines *when* fish will be *where*.

With the tides—particularly the flood tide—a movement of for-aging fish flows to and from the shores seeking the hundreds of sea animals that live near or upon the shore—small fish, shell fish, worms, crabs and sand eels. Besides, the constant action of the waves con-tinually pounding against the shores exposes other choice food bits.

To read the sea, get on a commanding point and scan the beach. Search for stretches of dark water indicating pockets and holes. If these are behind sandbars and reefs, they will "fish" decidedly better. Regardless of how good the hole is, it will be almost impossible to fish if you must cast across a sandbar. The sea runs strongest here and will wash your line and bait ashore. However, when it is behind the bar or reef, the waves will break upon the sand and dissipate their strength by the time they reach your fishing hole. Such locations often prove best, too, because bait fish and other small marine life will seek protection here, too, from the heavy running seas—and where there are little fish usually the big fish will follow.

From your vantage point look too for rocky places where kelp or some form of seaweed is growing within casting distance from the shore. Rocks are always good lurking places for fish, and I've yet to see a broken, rocky coastline that isn't productive. But mind the tides. Don't get yourself isolated on a rock with the tide coming in.

Deep water off points or jetties with fast-running currents and tide rips can be excellent locations, too.

Coastal spinning is usually best during a rising tide, but it can also be very good on the falling tide, outside of inlets where fish wait for food to be carried through the narrows.

As a result of this tidal action, fishing results may change rapidly. As the tide goes out or comes in, currents change, and a spot that is hotter than a pistol at high tide may be colder than a clam within an hour. If so, change location. Search for an inlet and cast into eddies and currents of the tide, just as you would a fresh-water stream. Work your lure alongside obstructions—on the shady side, preferably. If you are fishing the rocky wall of a river mouth, let your lure go down as you would in fishing a ledge in a lake.

Sometimes the surf caster can sight his prey and this is exciting. On calm days, with the help of Polaroid glasses—the darker the lenses the better—the angler may see snook, redfish, spotted weakfish and even tarpon cruising the coastal beaches. With practice, he can even pick out the species. Each fish has some pretty definite characteristics. In the southern waters off Florida, bonefish appear as ghostly shadows working into the shallow flats with the incoming tide, or they can be seen "tailing" as they bottom-feed, or they can be spotted by the bottom silt they stir up. Tarpon disclose their presence by rolling —a score of baby tarpon can create quite a commotion. The king salmon you'll spot by his leap and the slap of his broad tail.

If you're a salt-water spinman who takes to a boat, there are many surface "readings" to help you find your sport. Thousands of pairs of sharp eyes are aloft constantly to help you. Should you see a flock of gulls and terns wheeling, diving and screaming more than usual, the chances are they've discovered a school of fish feeding. Should they be bluefish, the gulls will strike it especially rich. These bloody marauders literally chop up an entire school of bait fish, providing choice bits of shredded fish.

In the absence of birds, should you see what seems to be a tiny shower of spray in the distance, close to the surface, close with it. It may well be the frantic leaping of a vast school of bait fish trying desperately to escape the slashing game fish underneath. If they are mackerel, run your boat slowly around the school and cast your lure into it. The mackerel will strike your streamer fly with such ferocity that they will imbed the hook beyond the barb and promptly bore down, ripping off line at an alarming rate.

As with reading any water, the important thing is this: Keep your eyes open and your mind working.

IV. TROPHY FISH

LANDING SPECIMEN FISH

The best of spinning comes now—making those belly-sagging lunkers say, "Uncle!"

Don't wait for one of those heavy fish to swing on and take the line sizzling off your spool before planning how to fight him; the time to prepare for the exciting occasion is right now while you're still calm, cool, and fairly well collected. With fine spinning tackle, the odds may seem to favor the big fish. Well, perhaps, if you haven't rehearsed your situations and discarded a lot of moth-eaten ideas on big-fish handling. If it's any help, remember that any accomplished dry-fly man isn't worth the salt in his beer if he can't handle a 5-pound rainbow on a 1X leader—and 1X is 1½-pound test which is lighter than any spinning line made. Besides, the dry-fly man hasn't a slip-drag clutch to neutralize his errors.

Given some experience in handling big fish and a fair shake, there is no reason why the spinman shouldn't be able to kill the largest fresh-water game fish made with his 4½-ounce rod and an 8-pound test line, or 6-pound test for that matter!

This is what is called for in big-fish handling: extracting the last ounce of strength from your light outfit—including the tying of modern knots; fighting your fish intelligently so that every second he is on goes toward exhausting him; and subjecting every accepted fish-

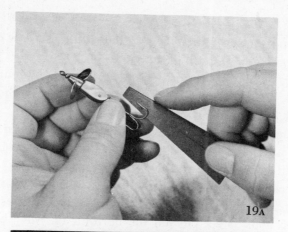

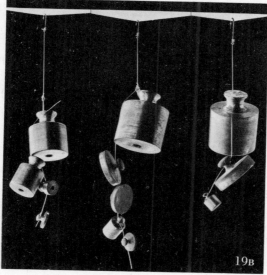

FIGURE 19. *Keep your hook sharp for easy penetration! (19A) It's very important to sharpen the hook every time it pulls over a rock or branch. Touch it up even after striking or playing a fish. Do the sharpening from the sides and inside. If the whetstone has grooves, don't use them because they may sharpen the hook on the wrong side. Remember, the sharper the hook, the easier it is to set it. Graphic evidence of the difference that sharpness makes in a hook (19B, below). Weights on the left—73 grams—show pull required to set a sharp No. 16 hook in a piece of bond paper. Those in the center—121 grams—show pull required if the No. 16 hook is dull. Those at the right— 122 grams—show pull needed for a sharp No. 10 (larger) hook.* Pictures used by permission of Outdoor Life.

fighting belief, however cherished, to the cold test—how does it help me take larger fish on my light tackle?

Among the ideas to test are these: "Always fight your big fish on a tight line," "Use a big hook for a big fish," and "The heavy rod will kill the big fish faster."

How many times, with a big fish on, have you been told: "Man alive, keep a tight line on that fish!" More often than not, that advice followed will lose you your big fish!

After considerable experimenting with slack lines, it is my contention that giving the broad-beamed lunker slack just as soon as the small sharp hook is set beyond the barb, at the very beginning of the fight, will save you that big fish more often than a tight line will. In fact, properly using a slack line will put more big fish on your wall than any other one thing you can do when fighting a fish!

The trophy fish's first reactions to a slack line, once the barb is set, is often quite comical. He seldom gets excited. If anything, he acts puzzled. He doesn't seem to know where to go. Usually, if he does make a run for it, he goes exactly where you want him: up the main channel of the river, away from the weed beds and the rapid water below you. Or, should he be excited for a moment, the slack line gives him nothing to fight against. Rushing 100 yards away from his favorite hold effects no release from that pesky hook in his jaw. To rid himself of the annoyance, he may make a leap, as does the occasional fish which has had a hook left in its face.

After the big fish has cruised the depths for a minute or two, tighten up gradually, playing him softly and gently. What happens? The great fish continues to swim back and forth in the deep water, unexcited, but yet wearing himself down. Then, as the fish slows, pour more strength into the battle. And then, finally, when he comes exhausted to the top, that's the time to give him just a little more pressure to lift his upper jaw as far out of the water as his great size will permit. While doing so, never fear, that wonderful slip-drag clutch will not allow you to overtax the strength of your line, providing that the line has not been weakened during the fight.

It's toward the end of the fight, when the battle goes into its final rounds, that the pressure must be maintained, because by then the hook may have worn a hole in the jaw and a slack line might let the hook drop out, the barb notwithstanding.

Of course the logical question is: "But won't a slack line let the fish throw his hook?"

Let's save that one until we've had a chance to discuss big hooks.

There is such a thing, of course, as getting down to too small a hook for your big fish—but I've yet to see the angler who errs in this direction. The usual fault is to fish with treble hooks or with hooks which are much too large.

In testing the penetration factor of small hooks as against larger, I found that a No. 16 hook took 73 grams to pull beyond the barb while a larger No. 10 hook took 122 grams. This means that the smaller hook slipped in beyond the barb at least one third more easily. However, when the small hook was dulled it took 121 grams to enter beyond the barb—just one gram less than the larger hook. (This, of course, points up a second important factor: keep your hook needle sharp at all times. See Figure 19.) From these tests, it is quite obvious that a small sharp hook will penetrate beyond the barb with less effort and will put a fish on the end of your line, while a larger hook might not get through the tough ligament at all.

As every careful angler knows, at least half of the fish landed will be hooked by a mere filament of skin. (Since I have been using smaller, sharper hooks and lighter rods and lines, my proportion of lightly hooked fish landed as against well-hooked fish is just about two out of three.) Now, if a large hook had been used, or if the fish had been snubbed up with a heavy rod or held in check with too heavy a line, the hook would have pulled through most of these lightly hooked fish—and the loss would have been explained: "Well, I only got a few bumps today. No real hits." Or: "Funny thing, all the fish seemed to be striking short."

To answer that hook-throwing question. Once a hook is set beyond the barb, contrary to popular belief, the fish cannot throw it. He just doesn't have such hook-throwing muscles in his head! (Besides, haven't you hooked up on your clothes often enough to know how exasperating it is to get the hook out? For that matter, I once caught a hook through my lip—and no amount of facial contortions could have thrown it.)

The hook will come out of the fish's face, sure enough, but only when the fish can exert enough pressure against your rod to tear it out or at least to tear a hole big enough so that the barb will no longer hold. What actually happens is that the angler's "tight line" usually jerks the hook out through the tiny filament by which it is held.

As mentioned before, most fish are lightly hooked. In the water, a 5-pound fish weighs about 4 ounces! When he leaps and gets his full length out of the water he automatically becomes 20 times as heavy! The same goes for a 150-pound man. When he gets into a swimming pool he weighs only $7\frac{1}{2}$ pounds and can support his weight by merely pressing against the bottom of the tank with his little finger. In salt water, he weighs even less. In leaping, the big fish usually makes tremendous contortions, swinging his broad tail from side to side, almost slapping his brains out. At such times, with pressure applied by the angler, certainly the hook can be pulled out—but not with the slack line.

What do the "tight-line" boys say who lose so many of their fish during the leap? "I didn't give him enough slack when he jumped!" That is all very well to say, but I have yet to see the angler who is fast enough to lower his rod every time the fish jumps.

Of course the tight-line expert has a good alibi which sounds foolproof when his knot parts. "He was mine. I had him under perfect control until he leaped and came down smack on my line and broke it!" With a slack line, of course, this excuse wouldn't be necessary—the fish, more than likely, would still be on.

There is no gainsaying, a big fish can dislodge a heavy lure by shaking his head during his leapings. If the fish is lightly hooked, the swinging lure's momentum might pull the hook out. But with our light spinning tackle, that lure is seldom large enough or heavy enough to be torn out by the fish's head-shakings. Also, I'd like to point out that every time I've seen a hook dislodged it invariably came flying back toward the fellow holding the rod. Rather odd, isn't it? You'd think, just once, that the fish would hurl it to the other side. May I raise the slight doubt, even with a heavy lure, that the angler might have had something to do with dislodging that lure?

Next, let's tackle the commonly held belief that a heavy rod will kill a fresh-water game fish more quickly than a light flexible rod. Often, the contrary is true—the light rod, properly handled, can bring the trophy fish to creel even faster than the stiff, heavy rod, and by heavy I mean one that is fully twice as heavy. In exhausting the great fish it is not the strength of the pull on the fish that does it—it's the action the fish is forced to make that wears him down—the long runs, the side-jarring leaps, the threshings—this, plus the constant tension brought to bear on him during these runs. This the light flexible rod can manage much better than the stiff, heavy one.

Should the great fish elect to go to the bottom and hang on, re-couping his strength as he does so, give him no quarter. Make him fight. Should he not respond to the tapping of the rod on a tautly held line, throw in a couple handfuls of gravel. That'll stir him. In keeping the fish fighting, don't underestimate the power of your light rod and spinning line. Test them out before you go fishing and find out for yourself what a difficult job it is to break the line on your rod—and yet that rod is capable of holding a powerful swimmer! See Figure 20.

Be prepared. The time will come when you play your trophy fish when he will make for some rapids, despite the braking power of your slip-drag clutch. There is one trick, and that alone, which may stop him. Lift the pick-up finger and give him slack. Don't keep an ounce of pressure on him. With the monofilament peeling off and ten-sion removed, he will seldom go more than a hundred yards, if that. Nine times out of ten, he will pause before he's gone fifty yards; the line will be carried below him by the current, and the light tension which the current creates on the line below him is enough to cause him to turn upstream toward the hole where you first hooked him and give you that heaven-sent opportunity to get below him and then tighten up, forcing him to take more vigorous upstream action.

Making your trophy fish fight an upstream battle saps his strength more quickly. In a four-mile-an-hour current, a fish which travels about eight miles an hour at top speed will be reduced to four miles an hour if he stays in mid-current, while if he were to go downstream he could merely keep upright in the water and exert an equal pressure on your outfit. Actually, by using his own top speed he could go twelve

FIGURE 20. *In fighting your first large fish, an apparent disadvantage may show up when you try to regain line. Because the slip-drag clutch has been set below the breaking point of the weakest knot in your line, nothing may happen when you begin turning the reel handle with the lunker on. In fact, despite your cranking, the big fish may even take more line out. That's fortunate—the slip-drag is working, guarding against overtension. (20A) In such a case, stop reeling because every turn of the handle when no line comes in puts from 3 to 4 twists into the line and will eventually break it. Instead of reeling, pump your fish in. Raise the rod tip, then lower it quickly and reel in the slack. To increase your return, step back as you raise the rod and come forward as you lower it. (20B) Should you return your large fish, do not let him float into the swift current belly up. Rather support him upright in the water. Recovered, let him glide out of your hands into the deeper water. You'll feel singularly elated as he swims away to fight you again on a day when the odds won't run against him.*

miles an hour. Four as against twelve miles an hour makes quite a difference to the angler.

Should he be a stubborn fish and elect to go into the weed beds despite your slack line, give him five minutes to back out. If he doesn't, slowly put on some pressure and relax the tension again. After two attempts, one such fish obligingly backed out of a muskrat hole for me. But should your fish not perform the third time, you'll have to begin balancing up whether his size justifies wasting any more good fishing time.

There will come the time, of course, when you will hook into the outlaw—the fish who will not be stopped while his heart beats. When you hook such a fish, let him go, following as best you can with your rod high in the air and hi-yi yipping, enjoying your good fortune while you have it. As the spool cleans, you'll be thankful for that 99-per-cent knot which holds the end of your 4-pound line to the spool. The best you can do is hope the knot will hold and that the line will part in the knot nearest the fish. If not, well, wasn't it worth being cleaned by a rip-snorting outlaw who simply would not be stopped? Besides, that is why you carry two extra full spools whenever you go where there are big fish stirring.

Thoroughly exhaust your big fish before trying to bring him to hand. Take the few more minutes to wear him down completely. Many a partially exhausted big fish has gained his freedom at the landing: few weak ones.

Theory behind, let's step into action. When the big fish hits, set the small, sharp hook gently. Then, release all tension as you storm out of the water, right now, to prepare for some fancy footwork, if necessary. If you are in a boat, flip the anti-reverse "on" to leave your left hand free. Up-anchor, get the motor started, get all other lines out of the way, and be ready to chase him, if need be. It's a comforting thought now, isn't it, to know that the finer the line you used, the longer the backing on your spool?

Next, figure out where you can play the fish to your best advantage—not his—preferably in slower, shallower water and if possible where there is a sloping beach. Should the heavy fish elect to go downstream to another pool, or even a fourth or a fifth, reshape your plans accordingly.

If you can, get below him. Gradually, begin to pour on the heat and let him know that you are master.

Eventually, with careful handling, even the biggest fish in the stream will become tired and thresh freely on the water's surface. Remain as quiet as you can; then you will not alarm the incoming fish. As he floats in, spent, reach down with your right hand and work it over the great fish slowly, avoiding his sensitive median lines—those narrow stripes running down the middle of either side of the fish where nerve ends come out through tiny holes in the scales. With your hand over him, press together your thumb and forefinger over the gills, take a tight grip and lift the heavy trout or salmon out of the water. Pike or muskies which have been played on a light 6-inch wire leader may be picked up by a grip of thumb and forefinger into the eye sockets. Bass can be lifted by putting your thumb inside the open mouth and gripping with the bent forefinger under the lower jaw.

If the fish is too large for lifting, back up slowly on a shallow sloping beach, at least twenty feet from the fish, and slide him steadily up the gentle-sloping beach with his own feeble tail floppings helping to beach him.

V. BUILDING YOUR ROD

ASSEMBLING A SPINNING ROD

Few things equal the quiet pride an angler takes in killing a trophy fish on his own homemade rod.

Besides providing a pleasant set of evenings, the building of the rod gives the spinman the chance to make just about the kind of glass rod he wants and, equally gratifying, saves himself money in doing so.

The following instructions have been boiled down to minimum essentials—yet, followed, they will produce a splendid, serviceable rod.

These are the things you will need: (1) hollow glass rod blanks complete with cork grip, metal bands and the middle ferrule. (2) A matched set of graduated spinning guides. (3) A tip top. (4) Wrapping thread—silk or nylon. (5) Rod cement. (6) Color preservative. (7) Rod varnish. (8) Fine wire wool. (9) Scotch tape, adhesive or rubber bands. (10) The following miscellaneous items: a piece of chalk, some books, a pocket knife, a razor blade, and a short length of thread.

Most sporting-goods stores can supply these things. If you cannot get the spinning rod blanks to suit your needs, complete with cork handle, middle ferrule and metal reel seat bands, may I suggest that you write directly to these two hollow glass rod blank manufacturers:

Pacific Laminates, 1550 Superior Avenue, Costa Mesa, California, and R. L. Winston Rod Co., 684 Harrison Street, San Francisco.

There are several good spinning guides on the market—the lightest is a hard chrome-plated wire "Foulproof" guide made by the Aetna Manufacturing Co., 2636 Ontario Street, Burbank, California. These guides flex with the rod but they must be treated carefully. More rugged guides, but heavier, are made by W. W. Mildrum Jewel Co., East Berlin, Connecticut, and Perfection Tip Co., Box 13, Capitol Hill Station, Denver, Colorado. The gathering guide should stand at least ⅜ inch off the rod blank and the succeeding guides should have a correspondingly high saddle, lessening toward the tip top, which must also be offset at an angle to reduce friction.

The lighter the rod the finer the wrapping thread I like to use, but this is a matter of refinement. If you use nylon, get a size from A to E; in silk from OO to EE. See Figures 21-24 for how to assemble a rod.

After you have made your rod, you'll want to take good care of it. To protect the rod and its high-standing guides, carry it in a hard case and never jam it in. A soft, compartmented cloth case will protect the rod against marring and scratching inside the rod case. Be sure the inside edge of the top of your case is smooth—otherwise in taking your rod out you may scratch its fine finish.

If you treat your rod well—wiping it after you get through fishing, particularly the metal parts after each salt-water trip—it will give you a lifetime of good spinning.

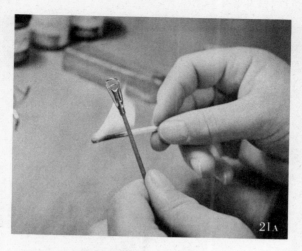

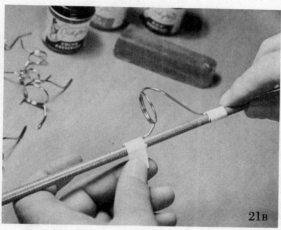

FIGURE 21. *To assemble a rod, first put on the tip top (21A). For a glass rod, use plastic cement. Read the instructions on the bottle and then fit the cement and the heated tip top into place. I prefer a reinforced chrome-plated tip top instead of agate, which is more expensive and heavier. Cheaper, imitation agate guides crack quite easily. Should you be making a combination fly and spinning rod which has a reel seat at the end, attach your fly reel and then be sure the tip top and gathering guide line up with the reel seat. Space your guides correctly. Incorrect size and placement can reduce your distance by 30 per cent.*

Tape on your large gathering guide first (21B), from 19 inches to 23 beyond the top of the cork grip. This guide must have sufficient distance from the reel spool to permit the line to "balloon" and have a saddle high enough to prevent line slapping.

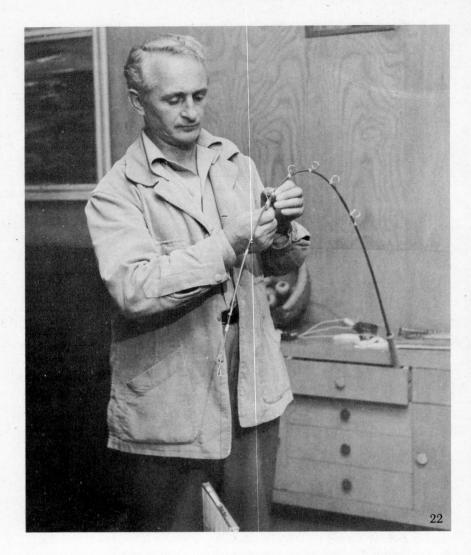

FIGURE 22. *The secret in placing the remaining guides is to prevent the line from touching the rod when it is flexed. Because no two rods—either bamboo or glass—bend exactly alike, the guide spacing will vary. To do this properly, anchor the butt of your rod at a 45 degree angle. Then hang a weight from the tip. On the back of the rod, tape on the matched guides progressively closer toward the tip so that a line pulled taut through these guides will not touch the rod. Rubber bands can be used, too.*

It may be necessary to bend the guides slightly so that the feet will fit flat on the rod. File or hone sharp edges on the top surface of the feet of the guides to eliminate the danger of cutting your wrapping threads.

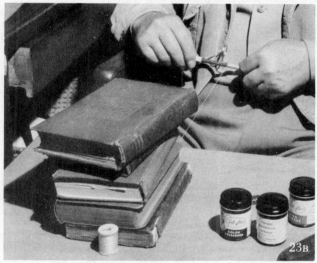

FIGURE 23. *Align the guides with the tip top (23A). Make adjustments where necessary. Perfect alignment is highly desirable. The angle of the camera is deceptive. The closer guides, of course, are much smaller.*
(23B) Place the thread spool behind an old book, preferably your well-read copy of The Compleat Angler. *Open the book and pull off about 2 feet of wrapping thread and insert it between the pages and close the book. Pile up additional books to increase the thread tension until it suits you. Place the rod across a chair's arms and you are ready to start wrapping. A few practice turns will determine the right thread tension.*

FIGURE 24. *Start by wrapping over the end of the thread toward the guide so that the thread end is held down by the wrapping (24A). Wrapping from in front of the guide and up over the guide's foot will give you the best wrap. To get a smooth wrap at the tip top you may wish to wrap double— that is, wrap toward the tip top and then double back. Using the tension from the books to hold the wrappings tightly, continue to turn the rod so that each thread lies as close as possible to the preceding turn. Five turns from the finish of the wrap, insert the loop of a tie-off thread, a 6-inch piece of slightly heavier thread. Finish the wrap over this tie-off thread. Holding the wrap tightly, cut off the wrapping thread about 4 inches above your rod and insert this cut end through the tie-off loop. Still holding on to the wrapping thread, pull smartly on both ends of the tie-off thread. This will put the wrapping thread under the wrap. Pull it up fairly tight.*

For a custom-built appearance, add a trim. A neat job can be done by starting the trim wrap against the wrap and winding away from it. For balance, confine these trim wraps to ten turns. Five is better. Insert the tie-off thread at the start of the trim wrap. Don't overdo the trim. That will make it look amateurish.

(24B) With the back of the knife blade or your thumbnail, push the wrapping up solid so that the rod or guides do not show through. Pull up again on the thread ends and trim them off very closely with a razor blade, being exceedingly careful not to cut into the wrap.

(24C) After sighting down the rod again, to make certain that the guides are in perfect alignment, give the wrappings a coat of color preservative. Without it, varnish dulls the thread's color. Be sure the preservative penetrates into the crevice formed between the wrap and the guide feet. A wonderful home-made preservative is one part Duco household cement to one part amyl acetate. To finish, apply several coats of rod varnish to all wraps. This can be done best with your thumb and forefinger. Fingers minimize the tendency of air bubbles to form in the finish.

Five thin coats are better than one or two heavy coats. To lay it on thin, dip the face of your dry index finger into the rod varnish, then press your thumb and index finger together to coat both surfaces. By rotating the wrapping between these surfaces a very smooth thin coat can be applied.

When the first coat is thoroughly dry, work it down gently with fine steel wool. Be sure to get these tiny wool fibres off the wrappings before you apply your next coat of varnish.

For a super-special job, hand-rub your blanks with a pumice-and-water paste or with fine steel wool before mounting the guides. Then, after the guides are wrapped, ink your name, address and the rod's length and weight on the rod in tiny script. Then varnish the whole rod.

If it is a bamboo rod you are autographing, scrape the varnish off the surface, put on a thin coat of color preservative, and then ink in your name —otherwise the ink will run on the bamboo.

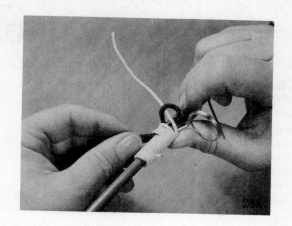

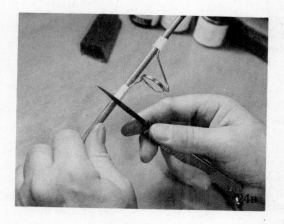

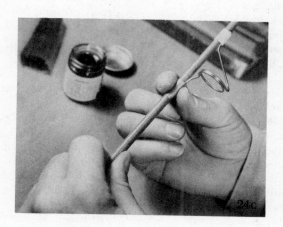

INDEX

French nylon, 28, 29

Gantron (*see* flies)
Garcia, Charles & Co., 64
German nylon (*see* platyl)
gravel, 83
Grey, Hugh, 8
grip, cork (*see* handle)
guides, 21, 25, 27, 57, 87-92
gut, 61, 64

handle, 21, 22, 87, 89
Hardy (reel), 20
Harnell (rod), 26
hatch, 73-74
Heddon (rod), 26
hooking the fish, 27, 60, 85
hook penetration, 79-82
hooks, 32, 36
hook sharpener (*see* whetstone)

keel, 32, 36
knots, 8, 64-66, 78
    blood, 57, 61, 64
    double-eye, 65, 66
    double loop, 64
    dropper, 61
    figure eight, 64, 65
    jam, 64
    loop, 61, 64
    ninety-nine per cent, 59, 85
    overhand, 59
    perfection loop, 63
    slip, 65
    Turle, 57, 65, 66
Kolzer, John, 58
Kreider, Claude, 8

lake currents, 72
lake fishing, 52, 53, 54, 70-75
landing the fish, 86
leader, 8, 24, 28, 57, 66, 78
Leonard (rod), 26
line, 8, 18, 24, 25, 26-29, 56,
    60, 66, 76
    backing, 29
    color, 29
    twist, 32
Long, Jay, 8

lure, 8, 21, 24, 25, 27, 30-37
    box (*see* box)
    polishing, 32, 69
Luxor (reel), 20

mackerel, 25, 77
Masterreel (reel), 20, 26, 31
McClane, Al, 8
McDermand, Charlie, 8
Metro (reel), 20
Mildrum, W. W., Jewel Co., 88
minnows, 30, 32, 36, 49
Mitchell, Jim, 8
Mitchell line (*see* French nylon)
Mitchell (reel), 20, 26, 31
momentum (*see* casting)
Monti (reel), 20
Mucilin (fly dressing), 58
muskellunge, 28

netting a fish (*see* trophy fish)
noise (*see* sound)
nylon, 26, 61, 64
    braided, 26
    monofilament, 20, 26, 28
nymph (*see* flies)

optic (*see* flies)
Orvis (rod), 26
overhead cast (*see* casting)
overholding, 8, 20, 84
overstriking, 8

Pacific Laminates, 88
Payne (rod), 26
Pecos (reel), 20
Pelican (reel), 20
perch, 35
Perfection Tip Co., 88
Phillipson (rod), 26
pick-up, 18, 49, 51, 83
pike, 28, 35
platyl, 26, 27, 28, 29, 61, 64
playing a fish (*see* trophy fish)
Plucky (lure), 32
plug, 8, 30, 36
Polaroid glasses, 76
preservative color (*see* color preservative)